REPLACING THE RED PENCIL

BY
GEORGE FRANKLIN ROSSELOT

Replacing the Red Pencil
Copyright ©2006 by George Franklin Rosselot
Tallahassee, Florida ~ All rights reserved.

ISBN #0-9779579-1-8

Printed in the United States of America. All rights
reserved under International Copyright Law.
Contents and/or cover may not be reproduced
in whole or in part in any form without the
express written consent of the author and publisher.

Cover Design by Mim Davis

Irving, Texas 75062

"The more I know, the more there is to know
 – *how exciting life can be!*"

George Rosselot

TABLE OF CONTENTS

FOREWARD   7
PREFACE   11
DEDICATIONS   17
ACKNOWLEDGMENTS OF APPRECIATION   19

SECTION I
Our Current System   25

    CHAPTER 1 - Physical Survival   27
    CHAPTER 2 - Emotional Survival   35
    CHAPTER 3 - Survival Teaching Methods   41
    CHAPTER 4 - Survival Method Produces
        Miracles and Violence   47
    CHAPTER 5 - The Dilemma   57

SECTION II
A New Model for the 21st Century   61

    CHAPTER 6 - Listen!   67
    CHAPTER 7 - Add On (Batting Averages)   75
    CHAPTER 8 - Be Efficient and Effective   79
    CHAPTER 9 - Be Response- "Able"   81
    CHAPTER 10 - The Actualization of
        What You Know   87

SECTION III

Guideline for Maintaining a Firm Footing in A World Where Change is Constant   97

CHAPTER 11 - Fair-Mindedness and Equality   101
CHAPTER 12 - Life is Made for Me   107
CHAPTER 13 - Win-Win   109
CHAPTER 14 - The Spiral of Vulnerability   113
CHAPTER 15 - Take Charge!   119
CHAPTER 16 - Concentrate on the Positive   139
CHAPTER 17 - What to Do Now!   143

APPENDIX A - LISTENING   145

APPENDIX B - CHANGING IRRATIONAL "SELF-DOWNING" TALK TO RATIONAL "SELF-APPROVAL" TALK   155

APPENDIX C - RULES, ROLES & BOUNDARIES   163

APPENDIX D - SCRIPTURE REFERENCES   165

APPENDIX E - ABOUT THE AUTHOR   167

FOREWARD

I have known George Rosselot for many years. At one point, I was in private practice with him at Eastwood Counseling Clinic here in Tallahassee, Florida. He established the clinic as a multidisciplinary practice of psychologists, psychiatrists, clinical social workers, marriage and family therapists, mental health counselors and counseling psychologists to meet the needs of individuals seeking therapy.

Mr. Rosselot has pioneered in many areas contributing to the health and well being of individuals seeking therapy. A few highlights of his accomplishments and special areas of expertise are his unique, practical, and therapeutic approaches relating to women's issues, concepts of marriage as a friendship, family roles and relationships as well as revolutionary concepts relating to the academic classroom and its role in modeling our youth and society as a whole.

He has also contributed to professional organizations as being President of the Florida Association of Marriage and Family Therapy

Foreward

(FAMFT), serving on committees for the American Association of Marriage and Family Therapy (AAMFT), and working extensively with the Florida Legislature to acquire laws for therapists in order to provide confidentiality and privileged communication for clients and their therapists.

Mr. Rosselot was honored as a Fellow by AAMFT for his legislative accomplishments establishing Marriage and Family Therapy as a profession by State Law. He received recognition for outstanding leadership at the AAMFT National Convention in 1986; was issued the first Marriage and Family Therapy license by the Florida Department of Professional Regulation (DPR) honoring his accomplishments with regard to the first licensing of Marriage and Family Therapists in the State. In addition, DPR, AAMFT administrators and various division leaders have called him on as a consultant over the years.

As a clinician in full time private practice, he has dealt with the complex issues where law, regulation, and intra-professional systems mesh at a grass roots level. He was one of the leaders and communicators to activate and design a Coalition of Interdisciplinary Professionals within the State of Florida. He has extensive understanding and experience in the political arena involving legislative and professional issues.

As a professional, I have known Mr. Rosselot to be constantly searching to contribute to others for their best interest and the best interest of society. He is a pioneer in his field and is now making a contribution to a larger audience through publishing what he has found to be helpful in providing new knowledge and insights for individuals to be able to live creative, productive and fulfilling lives.

I am fully aware of his concepts and am confident in their results. I feel they will make a difference and lead individuals to discover the true richness of everyday life.

Donald R. Bardill, Ph.D., LPSY
Professor Emeritus, Florida State University
Past National President,
American Association of Marriage and Family Therapists

PREFACE

Our education system needs to undergo a major overhaul. The Red Pencil teaching method in our classrooms is causing a rebellious and angry society. Change FIVE of the current teaching methods to FIVE non-punishment methods and you potentially change society. This book has current political implications, especially considering the debate on education within local communities, state legislatures, as well as Federal education issues and laws.

In spite of our societal upbringing, as individuals we can use these concepts to learn new ways to think, reprocess and reprogram our personal lives. It is my hope that this book will shed light on the current situation of our educational and parenting systems that have been in need of an overhaul for the past 30 years, as well as help those of us who went through this process to be more productive, to experience more creativity, and to live more courageously.

We need to share these same concepts with others in the hope of influencing and ultimately improving our lives today and changing future classroom methodologies of tomorrow!

INTRODUCTION

The change from the concepts of physical survival to the discovery in how we deal with emotional survival is what this book is all about. It is important to understand both physical and emotional survival systems and tools. By viewing the historical model of the academic classroom, one can better understand that a new teaching method is needed, which is better suited for today's physical and emotional survival versus our current method that is predominately founded on physical survival.

The primary method of instructing, teaching, and implementing discipline used by authorities for centuries and still used today is the use of punishment. The "I'll tell you what you do wrong" and punishment forms of discipline are not working in our current social system. Punishment is used to assure correct behavior for the best interest of the recipient. The result is a paradox. Some individuals become high achievers to avoid punishment. Others rebel and become passive resistant and, in many cases, lash out in anger. This is a major reason for our angry society. As society becomes more rebellious, punishment methods become more severe or at least more prevalent, and anger elevates further. Today, we

Introduction

are experiencing this at heightened levels. There is a need for a new definition of discipline combined with a set of tools, terms and concepts that are kind yet firm with understanding. These concepts provide a powerful contribution to all facets of our society. A new approach is greatly needed to effectively reduce the anger, rebellion, frustration, isolationism and confusion regarding interpersonal relationships.

There are five elements of this "Red Pencil" punishment model and teaching method that we need to replace. These are found in the first section of this book. The second section presents five approaches based on encouragement. The words "mistake" and "discipline" are given new meaning. This model is a new approach that uses natural consequences as opposed to punishment. The third section of this book concentrates on creative decision making, judgment, fair-mindedness and negotiating for a "win-win" outcome which provides the best results for individuals and society.

It is my hope, and has been my dream, that we change the academic classroom with a dynamic shift from just the basis of physical survival to include the necessary emotional survival methodologies within this teaching process. Although this process will revolutionize the historical system currently in place, it will take time to integrate the concepts within the classroom. However, it is imperative that this change be integrated as soon as possible. Not only should the integration provide and use new emotional survival tools, it must also make a fundamental change in a specific teaching method: the primary goal is to replace the "Red Pencil" punishment model.

I have had the opportunity to test these methods for over 40 years as an educator and psychotherapist. The results are miraculous and have the potential of reducing oppositional and violent behavior. The goal is to better develop each individual's potential, to create a cooperative and caring community and to enhance our current societal system.

This overall shift in teaching concepts is necessary for the stability, health, and well-being of individuals in our society. The hope is that each individual will have the tools to survive, become more productive, and be able to handle the constant changes of our current, multifaceted information age. In addition, individuals will also have a better understanding of approaches to being kind, firm, understanding (pursuing insights), and willing to deal with life in its simple, yet complex form. And to care about life itself.

In his many years of experience as a psychotherapist, George Rosselot has collected overwhelming evidence to support his contentions about what isn't working in contemporary relationships. In an effort to help his clients, he has carefully constructed working models of marriage, families and interpersonal relationships that evolve beyond the traditional model based primarily on physical survival. His concepts and methodologies are essential in that they better prepare his clients to accept the realities of their situations while also greatly shorten the time necessary for them to achieve a whole and healthy relationship. It is Mr. Rosselot's hope that his books will also help eradicate the disease of divorce and family decay by providing the general public with these proven concepts that have worked for his clients for over 30 years.

DEDICATIONS

I dedicate this book to
SHIRLEY MARIE ROSSELOT,
my wife and very best friend.
During these fifty-four years that we
have been married, she has always
been there encouraging and supporting
me in ways that if stated would
fill volumes of books.

ACKNOWLEDGMENTS OF APPRECIATION

To my FOUR CHILDREN: Michael Rosselot, Miriam "Mim" Davis, Marsha Thomas, and Merrilee Spears. Their lives from birth to the present have inspired me to always be in touch with each moment life presents. Occasionally it took quite a bit of courage living with their creative inventiveness!

To my FRIENDS AND TEACHERS who have been a part of my life adding to these concepts, knowledge, insights, and my personal growth and development.

To my FATHER AND MOTHER: Glen and Grace Rosselot, who gave me a marvelous heritage and a very enriched exposure to life. They were missionaries in Sierra Leone, West Africa. My father was principal of the Albert Academy, a mission high school of 40 to 50 young men. Many of these men after World War II came to the United States for their advanced degrees and established careers resulting in worldwide contributions.

Some of these men include Dr. John Karefa Smart. He became Assistant General Counsel

Acknowledgments of Appreciation

with the World Health Organization. I knew him when I was a boy and he was a student at the academy. We are still in contact with each other. He now lives with his wife Reena in Maryland. We talk and see each other often. Richard Caulker and his brother Soloman Caulker, Margi, and especially Warati and his wife Mary were a few of the individuals with whom I've been in contact over the years. Mary worked in our home when I lived at the Academy and took care of me as I grew up. Warati and Mary later married.

I don't want to overlook Bo-Bo, my childhood friend. Once he encouraged me to go without clothes as he did. Not wanting to be different, I immediately took off my clothes and continued to play. Later I went home without my clothes indicating that I was now a part of being an African little boy. My parents very kindly let Bo-Bo know that while it was all right for him not to wear clothes, George was still to wear his clothes. The memories of all the adventures I had in Africa with Bo-Bo are wonderful and priceless.

To my SISTER, Eleanor Laura Frances Luhman, who played a major role in my life. Growing up together in Freetown, Sierra Leone, we became very close and in tune with each other. I

Acknowledgments of Appreciation

learned about girls/women from her, especially how to respect and treat them. She often indicates that I was the "good kid" and she got all the blame. She also reminded me that I was very mischievous, and that I always seemed to find a way to get by with it.

I'd like to give my thanks to Barbara Lineberry. Barbara provided excellent proofreading. Barbara has worked with visually impaired people for many years and has read and put many textbooks on tape. She has proofread and been editorial assistant for a variety of sources over the years. And thank you to my eldest daughter Mim for countless months of transcribing, editing, organizing, designing and publishing this book.

For general support I'd also like to recognize my colleagues who sent letters of endorsement and have encouraged me to write these concepts to share with others. Special thanks go to Reubin O'D. Askew, Governor of Florida (1971-1979), Representative Everett Kelly, Florida House of Representatives for 22 years, Dr. Robert Miles, Psychiatrist, and Donald R. Bardill, Ph.D., LPSY Professor Emeritus, Florida State University and the Past National President, American Association of Marriage and Family Therapists.

Acknowledgments of Appreciation

And again, to Shirley, my loving wife and eternal friend. Shirley has opened my eyes to understandings I would have never known were it not for her sharing and caring for me. Knowing her as a person and woman has been the primary source for my knowledge and insight regarding the nature of women. I learned from her what it really means to be "ONE WITH EACH OTHER." She is the GREATEST GIFT OF MY LIFE. She is TRULY GOD GIVEN!

And most importantly, I am thankful to the Almighty God, the Creator, who gave me wisdom, discernment and insights to share with others.

SECTION I

Our Current System

Over the many years that I have been an educator and school guidance counselor, and since 1973 in private practice as a psychotherapist working with families and individuals of all ages, the one item that stands out over and over is what I call the "Red Pencil" punishment model.

In a short summary, it appears that the academic classroom teaching method is one of the major sources where the red pencil is used. It contributes both to miracles and violence. You ask, "How can this be?" Well there are five teaching approaches that the academic classroom uses. Parents and others follow this, too. However, the educational system is where we might make the greatest impact for change. If we can change the one major system that reaches all people, we have a chance of changing the entire social system.

CHAPTER 1

Physical Survival

The academic classroom teaching method is based on physical survival. For centuries, we as a race had to deal primarily with physical survival. Physical survival tools, terms and concepts are quite different from emotional tools, terms and concepts. Physical survival concepts include shoulds, shouldn'ts, musts, ought to's, you better, you better not, and were necessary for the survival of people. Interestingly enough even today, if it is a physical survival problem, these shoulds, shouldn'ts and ought to's still apply.

Within the academic system there is a specific model of teaching that is founded on the historic guidelines of physical survival. There are five factors in this physical survival (historic) method. In a classroom a process goes something like this:

Chapter 1

Teacher tells, student listens, teacher tells you what you do wrong, you are disciplined (to be sure you don't make the mistake again), and then you must be responsible and do what you should do (according to the authority—the teacher).

Included in this process is a statement meant to keep the student humble: *"the more you know, the more you find out, the less you know,"* therefore don't go on thinking you know everything.

The following provides a further explanation of these survival theories:

The Telling Model

The teacher *tells*, the student *listens*, and then the student *tells* back. If playback is exact (perfect) then student makes 100%. This is the "perfection" model. This produces the "listen/tell" response. You most often listen up to the point where you think you know the answer and immediately *tell* back. The result is that while the other person is *telling*, you are processing what you believe is the correct answer, rather than truly listening to the other person

Physical Survival

and "hearing" what they are saying. Remember? The first student with a hand up with the right answer gets an "A"!

The Red Pencil!

This is based on all that you do *wrong* and how to be *right*. The teacher tells what the student did wrong. The student corrects the problem and is then "right." *Plus*, the teacher tells the students how to correct what they have done and will also tell them how to improve. If the student is wrong, he or she is "less than" a person. It is important to add we are taught not to dwell on what we know, but instead to focus on correcting our mistakes and wrong answers and behavior.

The Punishment Model

It is good to correct your wrong doing (or wrong answers); however, it is still necessary to punish you (keep you after school) to be sure you do not repeat the wrong. To let you "get by" without some form of punishment is to risk your not viewing life as a serious business; thus, to be punished immediately now is better

Chapter 1

than to risk being wrong in the future and getting hurt later. This model is also "supposed" to prevent you from becoming careless, egotistical or disrespectful. This prevalent teaching model is contributing to the violence within our schools and our society. People are tired of being told what they are doing wrong, and many times some people will rebel and consequently passively or actively "act out" in passive or aggressive behavior.

The Authority "Knows"

When correcting or listening the student *must* have a very reliable authority to validate *when* the student is right. The system we currently have makes it very important for all authority figures to be seen as specialists in their field. Therefore, the authority must be right and be responsible. The authority assumes the role of being "right" and MUST maintain omniscience. The authority claims it has the right knowledge and will not be *wrong*. Therefore students and parents are the ones who fail, teachers and schools do not!

The Humility Model

Students must learn "the more I know, the more I find out, the less I know." It is important to realize that you are small and insignificant and really "less than" compared to the universe and creation itself. In order to correct old incorrect knowledge, it is necessary to admit former ignorance and then to be willing to forge ahead to demonstrate being corrected, even if under ridicule or being "put to the test." This model also requires the individual to go back to any of the above principles, willingly, with an attitude of remorse, submission, confession and above all, asking for forgiveness. If you correct old knowledge, it is necessary to admit your ignorance (stupidity) and then be willing to change and forge ahead, even while under ridicule or persecution.

Now consider these factors: telling you what you did wrong, punishing you, instructing you to strive to be perfect (as spelled out by the "perfect" authority) and teaching you to accept your punishment. Under correction (the Red Pencil) and punishment (and ultimately guilt), this model demonstrates to the authority that you have the willingness to accept your punishment in a humble way and ability to return to the classroom to do what you *should* do. This then proves that the student is being responsible and can appropriately follow and learn from the authority (the teacher). But that is not all; it must also be understood and portrayed by the student that he or she doesn't know everything since it is not possible to know everything. Be it ever so humble, the student must acknowledge the fact: "the more I know the less I know" therefore preventing a "swelled head". This statement is what the authority expects and demands from the students. The willingness on the part of the student to admit a mistake and not knowing everything is what is necessary for the teacher to understand, so that the student can show the acknowledgement of this fact, which is necessary for survival.

All of this sounds well and good and it has worked for centuries. And this still works in a physical survival system. Case in point – if you were in a military situation and on the front lines and you were instructed at a certain hour to begin to charge forward, it probably would not be in the best interest of everyone to stop and say, "Well do we really feel like doing this?" or "Do we really want to do this?" and "Are you sure that it is going to be OK for us to charge forward, couldn't this get us shot or killed?" No, when you are in a physical survival system you had better determine what the action is, make sure it has validity, and do it!

Another illustration would be how you enjoy getting up in the morning to feed the animals, take care of the garden, plow the fields, and make sure that everything is in order for one's well-being. However, if you were to hear wolves in the nearby woods, it would be important to hurry into your cabin, shut and bar the door and protect everyone. The last thing one would do in a case of survival would be to think and therefore act on a thought such as "I don't feel like shutting the door because I don't feel like going in right now. It is a beautiful day with a nice warm breeze." Most people wouldn't worry about how they *feel* about it. Most feelings and perceptions are tied into emotional survival. So, yes, it is still true today that physical survival methods and teachings must be learned. If you are not surviving physically, you are unable to do anything else.

However, today we have so many technologies and so many discoveries related to

Chapter 1

physical survival that we almost take it for granted until something happens. Instances that remind us that we must take care to survive would be like our driving in a car and someone swerves in front of you. Physical survival is still an important factor. We are reminded of physical survival as we continue to research to find cures for cancer, HIV-AIDS, and so forth. We must practice things like good nutrition, exercising and taking care of our health, drinking enough fluids, getting a good night's rest, making sure we have shelter and warmth. These are all things that we *should* do.

The problem we currently have is that now that our physical survival is more assured, our emotional survival needs to be explored and developed.

CHAPTER 2

Emotional Survival

Emotional survival is not a new era. About 2,000 years ago there was a man that looked around and saw the pyramids. He saw that fire and the wheel had been invented, industrialization was beginning, changes in transportation, shipping, and many societal events were taking place. Because of His wonderful knowledge and "knowingness" He understood that a few thousand years from that time, people would need another set of concepts. They would need to understand concepts related to emotional survival. And so He began introducing ideas of love, like "love thy neighbor as thyself."

There are many writings that talk about loving others and caring for others and taking no thought for yourself. But there are two basic things He said that were very important and these two concepts, two new laws for humankind, were set forth: To "Love the Lord your God with all your heart, mind and soul" and also to "love thy neighbor as thyself." These key concepts are the basis for emotional survival. If you consider the relationships between ourselves, our God, and others, these concepts provide the foundation that helps us in every aspect of positive emotional thoughts, actions and survival. However, we downplay the part about "as thyself." We are to love our neighbor as much as we love ourselves.

It is important that I take a moment to emphasize this point. This concept is a central element that plays heavily in the context of this book. Not only is it difficult for some to understand that it is okay to love themselves, but our society and its authorities do much to destroy any possibility of some considering themselves worthy of this truth. Many authorities say that loving yourself is to be selfish, self-centered, and egotistical. Granted, there needs to be healthy balance, however, it is necessary to acknowledge the importance of *knowing* and caring about ones' self in order to live a creative and contributing life.

For those who question their own self-worth and therefore have difficulty loving themselves, consider this: God created the universe, the world, and all that is in it. Then he created the human being in His own image. When you think about this you really are a miracle. Just take your physical self and think about everything from how you are put together with the billions of cells, veins and arteries, muscles, bones, and everything in between. All of these parts are put together in marvelous form and for incredible function. Think about your brain and its complexity which processes the various facets of your physical self. Then consider your mental thought processes, your memory, not to mention the multiple ways of learning, thinking and doing. Add to all of this the fact that we are also connected with God, communicating with God in a meditative and spiritual way.

We are also connected together as human beings in a supernatural way as well. We may call it Extra Sensory Perception, or ESP or mental telepathy. Sometimes we might be thinking about somebody else – they actually pick up on it. I've had times when one of my children called me and said "What do you want Dad?" and I had been thinking about that child. Just consider all of this (and so much more) ... we are miracles, each of us. We are one of a kind, every individual is unique. This "goodness" can only be the result of a marvelous, wonderful Creator.

When you really think about it, just the miracle of birth, your birth, is an incredible event. I had the opportunity to see our first child born and it touched my heart so deeply that I have held it as precious all these years. When you think of loving yourself you are really acknowledging that you are created by God and are precious in His sight. Put yourself into action and live your life with love not only for others, but also yourself. You will live a life of fullness and your potential is unlimited! Let love be your greatest aim, even as it applies to yourself.

These two commandments as stated by Jesus set forth the whole system for the era we are in now, where emotional survival is the predominant factor. This message is centuries old but it has even become more relevant now.

Chapter 2

The fact is we are pioneers all over again. If you take a look at it – when you think of emotional survival – perception is a key factor to emotion. Each person's perception is their own reality which in that sense means every person is right. To illustrate, try to tell someone he/she doesn't feel a certain way. The response would be "Well, that's how I feel. Don't tell me that I don't feel that way." And then you might say, "Anybody in their right mind doesn't and shouldn't feel that way". The response would then be "Are you telling me that I am not in my right mind?" ... and you go on and on in circles. No one will convince the other which one is right. The fact again is perception is each person's belief as to what is correct. These personal observations can go back to childhood, how we view our world, how tall we are, how short we are, whether we are male, female, blonde or brunette, children or adults.

There are varying reasons as to how we see the world. How the world sees us is also how we make our decisions as to how we are going to see the world. Again, although this process has been continuously evolving over the past centuries, we are still pioneers in this emotional survival era *and* in a much more complex, stressed, and crowded society.

The change from the concepts of physical survival to the discovery in how we deal with emotional survival is our theme. It is important to understand both physical and emotional survival systems and tools. By viewing the historical model of the academic classroom one can better understand the teaching method that is far better suited for physical survival versus today's much needed emotional survival.

CHAPTER 3

Survival Teaching Methods

The "telling" model has been the historical model which includes lectures and telling. This is necessary because people need information. The students are supposed to listen, do what they are told, and follow-through.

It is *important* to the teacher to tell you what you do wrong, because the logic is, *if* you are told what you do wrong, and you correct it, then you will be right. This is the obligation and the duty of the authority. It is also important that the teacher give you consequences of some sort, a penalty, because if you don't get punished, you won't pay attention. And so you have to have some kind of consequence like having to write 500 sentences. To let you "get by" without some form of reprimand is to possibly not have you see life in its serious form, to possibly have you get hurt in the future, or become careless, or worse – egotistical. It would also reveal that

Chapter 3

the teacher doesn't care about your well-being and toward being "right" or "perfect."

The problem with this process is that it is based on emphasizing of wrong-doing and rebuke. The "A" student consciously or unconsciously (mostly unconsciously) realizes this and so the "A" student does everything to be right to avoid any kind of punishment or being put down, or kept after school. All of this is very logical. But the interesting thing is, the "A" and most likely the "B" student many times is making these grades just to avoid punishment.

The "C-D" and especially "F" students who are always being told that they are wrong (with marks from a big old red pencil), get discouraged, upset, angry and out of rebellion or discouragement won't do their homework or participate. The "tell you" model creates great defense mechanisms on the part of the listener. Many times students skip school, they are mad because all they are learning is that everything they do is wrong. They are experiencing the Red Pencil punishment – which always tells them what they are doing wrong. A lot of these people are angry – yet they are often very creative people. They are tired of being told that they do wrong. But again... an "A" student may perform exceptionally because they see through this and they simply want to avoid punishment.

There are many illustrations of causes and effects of the Red Pencil. For example, during a football game a young man made a touchdown and had done an excellent job of getting through the defensive line. Later on the coach might say, "Good play, but just know that it is not always going to be that easy, and you probably should have handed off the ball to Bill and not been such a risk-taker and a show-off." In addition, the father would say, "Well that was great son, but just don't let it go to your head." These are Red Pencil marks. The goal is to never let children feel that they have completely accomplished something or they might rest on their laurels thinking everything is fine. The authority is obligated to always point out one more thing to correct.

By the way, Red Pencil is not just limited to students/teachers or parents/children. This principle occurs in all relationships. It is a learned technique from our academic past. A husband comes home from work and as the garage door opens, the wife comes out and hollers, "You take care of them. I am tired and I have had it." So he says, "fine" and he goes in and takes care of the

Chapter 3

children. Later, he comes out and finds that she is washing the car with a vigor that he can't believe. As he is standing there he says, "What are you doing?" and she says, "What's it look like?" And in order to *show that he cares* he says, "Well – you know you missed a few spots ... that's no way to wash a car." Amazingly, he can't understand why he got a sopping wet sponge thrown at him. The issue had nothing to do with washing the car; it had to do with getting out all of her frustrations and negative energy. These kinds of things are happening over and over and in the smallest ways, and unfortunately, in major ways.

There are all kinds of examples. A friend tells you how wonderful your child is but you reply, "Hold on, if you tell that to him he will become arrogant!" So much of emphasis is back to the Red Pencil. Always point out the smallest thing that you can think of because if you don't point out the little things that a person needs to improve, then it is as if you don't care as a parent, or care as a teacher.

If a teacher doesn't tell the students that they are doing wrong, the teacher appears not to care. Therefore the teacher would not be considering the welfare of the students and even possibly be thought of as not doing a good job. The Red Pencil methodology permeates through our society. Always tell a person – even if it is the smallest thing – what they could do better, because if you don't, you are letting that person get by. Notice how much easier it is for us to criticize. It is how we have been conditioned. The Red Pencil teaches us to find the mistakes, to highlight the problems, to seek and find everything that needs correcting. It is harder, because it is not taught as a part of our conditioning, to support each other. You have to be conscious of this practice, and it is more difficult. Developing a positive and encouraging attitude for others takes a higher level of patience and time, especially in the classroom – all because of our historic, physical survival, academic Red Pencil upbringing.

The intent, to be sure that everything is right, is one thing. But the fact is, we have moved into a much more complex society with emotional survival as a major factor. Therein lies the problem.

CHAPTER 4

Survival Method Produces Miracles and Violence

Miracles Within the Physical Survival Method

There is a miracle that occurs within this historical model. What happens are "A-B" students ultimately found they become achievers – they finally move on beyond fear of punishment and into feelings of success and accomplishment. These children are able to grasp the concept and after a period of several years, move out from under the punishment model to be productive and happy adults. These children eventually change from "avoiding" punishments to experiencing the positive reinforcements they realize from their successes. The shift from being motivated by negatives is changed to being driven to achieve because of the positive feedbacks and "add-ons" that they gain as they excel.

Chapter 4

Unfortunately, many of these people carry internal feelings of being afraid of making a mistake, fear of failure, and fear of consequences and inadequacies…for the rest of their lives. If someone isn't there to reprimand them, then all the voices and chatter boxes in their heads are telling them that they had better not do that, that they are wrong, and they must punish or discipline themselves so that they'll straighten up and do what is right. *(See Appendix B – Changing Irrational "Self-Downing" Talk to Rational "Self-Approval" Talk.)*

Another miracle that flows from this historic model is very interesting. At some point in time, the students that were upset with the Red Pencil (always being told what they did wrong) find out what all they really can do when they get away from the negative and punishment model. Some of these rebels, those students that were not the "A" or "B" students, end up becoming very successful entrepreneurs, computer gurus, teachers, surgeons, lawyers – even though they rebelled while in school. These particular students *determined* that they were not going to get chastised and humiliated anymore and so they worked out a way to change.

Again, unfortunately, many times these same people become the very people that inflict the

Red Pencil on others because the Red Pencil was inflicted on them.

Violence Within the Physical Survival Method

Some students, out of rebellion, learned how to "beat the system" and then they were able to achieve major accomplishments. They became successful just to show the authority that they could be achievers in "spite of the system." Others found something they could accomplish and moved on with their lives, again "in spite of the Red Pencil." They learned to stop self-punishment and moved on into marvelous inventions and amazing ways of contributing to themselves and to society.

But this is not usually the case. Many students that are tired of punishment and are tired of continually being told that they do wrong will eventually lash back at society in some form. Some forms are more serious than others. So, they think, "since I am being punished, I'll punish them." To try to get society to change and to stop punishing them, they turn around and essentially try to punish society by doing what society is doing. This becomes a vicious cycle.

Chapter 4

There are varying levels of violence with respect to the Red Pencil. You are always being told what you do wrong. Someone is pointing out that you do wrong. The results, as we mentioned, also become the voices in our head.

Susan Jeffers, Ph.D., the author of *Feel the Fear...and Beyond: Mastering the Techniques for Doing It Anyway* (Ballantine Publishing Group), wrote about those voices being "chatter boxes" in our head. These chatter boxes are there permanently for us to deal with because these are the voices of our historical past, basically the authority models. The way to catch these voices, or these chatter boxes, is to listen for words like should, shouldn't, ought to, have to, must, you better, or don't. These words are the triggers or the keys that bring up the Red Pencil.

Wherever there is one of these words (should or shouldn't) there is a very mild to major Red Pencil. Depending on the amount of what you do wrong and the degree to which you are told what you do wrong, the punishment received each time, at some level, minor to major, would be the degree to which you react to the should's or shouldn'ts. This brings up the fact that the Red Pencil goes back to our childhood. When a situation occurs in an environment where there is an authority figure or an implied authority (again greater or lesser), then it appears that the historical self-image of us, which Freud called the unconscious and Bradshaw called the inner child reacts to this. So if someone can make a very mild statement of "You should be on time and not be late" so many times, one inner child will cower and state, "I know, I'll try again." Another that had more powerful voices in their head might reply "You just don't understand" or "Leave me alone." Any kind of reaction to a telling model that tells you what you did wrong is the Red Pencil.

Our society has a high degree of anger. Many times in today's situations involving anger and violence we find that a person had a historical background of a major punishment model, to the point of cruelty. That person as an adult is going to be reacting much more to any "should" or *implied* "should" than the person who did not experience that extreme degree of punishment of the Red Pencil.

The authority model is to tell you what you do wrong based on historical physical survival, as I mentioned before, and this permeates our whole life. We go to work and we have people that are micro-manager supervisors telling us what we do wrong. And remember, teachers are not doing their job if they don't tell a student what they are doing wrong, and tell them what they should do, and reprimand them or give them a certain look of disapproval. So when we are in those positions of authority, or perceived authority, if we don't tell people what they are doing wrong, if we don't tell them like the Red Pencil does we are not doing our job. Yet we can't understand why the individual gets upset.

With all the stressors, economic and world issues, we are already under tremendous pressure; now add the issue "Am I going to be able to be right, am I going to avoid the Red Pencil?" Now there is an added and greater stressor compounding emotional survival.

This entire situation can get pretty complicated because of the fact that you have some people that came into the world that did not get any nurturing or bonding (which we call attachment disorder) and some children are born chemically dependent because their parents were drug or alcohol abusers. Mix all of these complications together, and any others you can think of then add in the shoulds and shouldn'ts and you can see why just one statement can cause a person to "go postal." This happens when one is "pushed to the wall." They are defensive and they panic. Desperate, they want to show they are right. Out of control and full of anger – their intent is to convince someone they are right – not to harm or dissent. So the alertness to the Red Pencil, and particularly if a person is highly sensitive to it, can produce all kinds of behaviors to the point of violence.

One of the things that I am very concerned with is when employers tell a worker that he/she is fired, may not return to work, and must pack up and leave. Some employers may even bring a security officer to the firing event. This is just asking for trouble, it creates the possibility for that worker to become very angry which could result in the fired employee harming people in the office or harming the employer. Many authorities find themselves in severe trouble and then have to become more of an authority in terms of increasing *control* thus increasing the punishment.

The word discipline may make you think of *control* in most instances. However, the root word of discipline is disciple. In situations such as parenting or supervising, those people that

Chapter 4

we parent are disciples. We choose the form and method to teach that disciple how to learn and understand. So if discipline is seen as controlling people using the Red Pencil that is one thing. But, if discipline is seen as ***discipleship*** to teach, to share, to help people get tremendous insight – that is much more effective and productive.

I counseled a young lady years ago who was in tears. She was making straight A's and was having difficulty with test anxiety. As we worked together one of the things I discovered is that she had a very strict father. One example is that she would sit at the dinner table and see something on her plate that she did not want to eat. In response to this, her father would put an extra portion of that particular food on her plate. In fact, at one time, he took some mashed potatoes and just splattered them on and around her plate. He then had her eat everything including licking up all the little splatters that were on the table. Finally he sent her to her room because she was not "minding." He didn't think what he was doing was wrong. He was just disciplining his daughter to correct her. The end result was her fear of making a mistake and being corrected which caused her test anxiety. Once she understood this, she was able to overcome her problem.

I've had other situations where a parent thought what they were doing was right. One parent was spanking his child every time he came home from school for years because the father said little boys always lie. So rather than asking how he did at school, the father spanked him every day. Talk about a very angry young man. One of the therapies that I used with that man was to go out into the woods and just let him scream and yell and throw and break dead sticks, etc. Some of his best friends were like strong oak trees – he loved the outdoors so he would never take an ax to a tree. Over time he worked out his anger and we got the violent behavior that was caused by his father, to stop. Interestingly enough you might guess what career he went into – he became a Forester.

So this idea of "watch out, everything is wrong" can trigger everything from your 2-year old inner child, to your 16-year old attitude, to any kind of situational factor that you reacted to in a minor to major way as a child. Add the historical self and the negative reaction can many times be predictable if you know that person's past or if that person knows his/her past. If someone has personally been in therapy, and has healed the inner child, this overcomes the Red Pencil. The process will change from "this is what needs to

Chapter 4

---

be done" to being able to discuss and negotiate therefore the inner child will not be controlling the situation.

Another issue that is rather shocking is that there is the McNaughten Rule of Law (1843) for insanity. There are various laws for insanity – but this particular rule states that one is insane and excuses criminal conduct of the defendant, as a result of a "disease of the mind" where the defendant: *(1) did not know the nature and quality of the act he was doing, or if he did know, (2) did not know that what he was doing was wrong.* This is a consequence based on the results of the Red Pencil.

CHAPTER 5

The Dilemma

How do we approach something that is not working? We approach it based on physical survival concepts when this particular behavior may be needed, however, we instead must emphasize the tools and concepts for emotional survival. This new emotional situation is different. So by using the physical survival methods (the Red Pencil) you are contributing to insanity be it in the form of pathology, delusions, anger, aggression, etc.

Put together all the emotional and societal stressors, the chemical stressors, the issues of health, and the heavy use of pharmacological drugs. Most psychotherapy treatments don't deal with the inner issues of people, especially pharmacological treatment. Add in constant change and super-technology, not to mention the stressors of the information age, and it becomes amazing that so many people are able to cope, deal and essentially perform the wonderful, marvelous, miracles that are done routinely on a daily basis. We have people successfully working in areas of science, philosophy, business, literature and music. Yet there are still the subtleties most productive people have learned: to avoid punishment and to avoid the Red Pencil.

Many people have learned that to be right is the priority instead of looking out for what is wrong. They *must strive to be right* (to avoid being in danger of being wrong). It's important to get beyond these internal chatter boxes, for then people will perform productive miracles.

Adler talked about a "mistake is a misdirected action because one didn't know what else to do at the time." Adler also said "guilt is all of those good intentions I never intended to do in the first place." Current belief is if you don't have guilt, then you don't have a conscience and you don't care, which could make you pathological. So it is important to have guilt so that you know that you are not pathological. In addition, this guilt demonstrates that you care and that you have a conscience. This, in turn, allows others to see that you are not pathological and that you do care. In unfortunate situations, some people carry guilt to an extreme. They use the energy found from guilt for purposes of punishment.

I think it was a great contribution for Adler to say if a mistake is made it doesn't mean you are bad, terrible, awful, or less than. Even though sometimes the mistake may be very severe, your willingness to find understanding and new answers to take on corrective action shows that you have a conscience and that you care. Using your energy to discover corrective action is much more productive than wasting your energy on guilt.

Let's list one more time the physical survival concepts. By telling you what you do wrong, you will be right, strive for perfection. Unless it is 100%, you are reprimanded, in one way or another, to ensure that you do what is right. And you must be sure that you don't assume that you know it all.

The problem is that this whole system is based on punishment. It is based on a *false* sense of humility (the more you know the more you find out the less you know). Therefore you can't claim to have all of the knowledge – because then you will be arrogant, egotistical and a know-it-all. You'll be a failure and you won't be humble – as society requires.

SECTION II

A New Model for the 21st Century

What is the new model? The one needed for today? It is an approach that encompasses and provides emotional survival. If basically five things were changed in the current academic classroom teaching method, over time we would have the potential to make a major change in our whole society.

The following provides an explanation of these new survival theories.

The Listening Model

Listen, and then listen again. Clarify words, nonverbal messages, situational implications or statements. Re-state, re-listen, and re-clarify. Gather feedback to see if speaker agrees. *(See Appendix A – Listening.)* This process must be learned. We tend to listen, but while we are listening we only listen up to the point where we think we know the answer and are immediately prepared to "tell" back. This results in while the other person is "telling" you are processing what you believe is the right answer, rather than truly listening to the other person.

Batting Averages – Add On

Determine what is known – and then what *else* you would like to know. This is a growth concept promoting creativity to place what one wants to know as a goal and to establish a "purpose for knowing" base as an enhancement toward your next forward move. This principle is a "add on" rather than correcting what is wrong.

The Efficient-Effective Model

Determine the level of efficiency one prefers or feels is necessary (depending on the survival level desired or mandated). The level you choose will be influenced by the survival level you need or that is required. This is the minimum standard. Your personal standard may be higher than the one required of you. Using this principle, if a mistake is made, "pick yourself up" and correct it; move on and "add-on" without punishment or guilt. A mistake has its own consequences. Punishment and guilt only waste time and energy. When you act out of your own best interest and you are your own best friend, you pave the way for others to act out of their own best interest and for them to be their own best friend.

The Response-Ability Model

It is important to set yourself up with the *ability* to respond, respond and respond. Promote the value of being (existing) instead of being (to just exist) by developing creative, growing and life enhancing behaviors. Preserving and nurturing the existence (being-ness) in others then becomes vital to your own existence!

The Actualization Model

The more I know the more I found out there is more to know – ***how exciting life can be!*** Change is constant therefore knowing is positive and essential to "being and becoming" in a creative sense. Humility is to be humane, have ego strength and self-esteem as you are always in search of new knowledge. To discover something new is to have come from a previous knowing or base of knowledge. One then moves from one base to a new base. Keeping the same base may also be new if it is kept as a result of new knowledge and the above models. Any decision is based on the criteria set forth in the "response-ability" model. This approach also provides "face saving" since you are always working from what is new. New knowledge (making decisions based on the knowledge and wisdom you currently have) does not make you less than or stupid. It instead affirms creativity and growth. *(See Section III – Guideline for Maintaining a Firm Footing in a World Where Change is Constant.)*

CHAPTER 6

Listen!

Historically the "tell you model" has been effective and is still effective in many situations, as mentioned before. But how else are you supposed to disseminate important information? Some of it is still "telling", but there are additional and more effective ways of communicating information.

One of the biggest problems with "tell-you" is the language. Our vocabulary has expanded tremendously. The ancient people, for example, may have had as few as 5,000 words in their vocabulary. There was only one way to tell someone something. This is one of the reasons why if you go back to ancient literature or ancient oral traditions (like the scriptures), people could tell a story over and over again and that story would last thousands of years and would never change because there was only one way in which to tell the story. This was simply due to the limitations of the vocabulary. A person could speak and with a limited vocabulary

Chapter 6

would be assured that whatever they said would be clearly understood. Even the tones of the voice would not have the variance in meaning as it does today. We now have more than 1,000,000 words in our vocabulary, with additional innuendos and non-verbal meanings. With so many ways to convey meanings, a speaker is not sure that he has chosen the most suitable one. Nor is he sure his listener has received it in the way he intended.

A very simple example would be to say the words "good night." These two words today could actually mean three different things (or more) depending on the circumstance in the inflection used by the speaker. The first could be a shortened version of simply saying it's been a good night (successful), as one closes out the accounting books of a restaurant at the close of business. Or the same words could be one's way of saying good-bye or see you later. However, these two words are also an expression of surprise or dismay in a similar way that good ol' Charlie Brown would say "good grief." But in earlier times it would have only been a means of expressing parting. In those days, what ever a person would say would be clearly understood, regardless of tones and inflections. The meaning would remain the same.

Listen!

Consider the knowledge explosion, which would include vocabulary as well. Kindergarten children in 1950 could use about 900 to 1,000 words on their own. They could understand 50,000 words in varying contexts and explanations. By 1980 kindergarten children could use 1,500 to 1,900 words on their own and could understand something like 80,000 words. This vast change was made possible, in part, by *Sesame Street, Electric Company,* and other television programs that were coming out that children began watching.

A good illustration of the words and meaning and listening skills we use today can be provided in a simple game of "telegraph." This game is where one person whispers a sentence to another person. This secret is then passed around the circle where 10 people are gathered. The last person tells everyone what the sentence is. It is usually very funny because it is not close at all to the first sentence spoken. The people in ancient days, with their limited vocabulary, could say a sentence to thousands of people over many years and the sentence would never change. This is also an explanation as to how stories and history were passed down so accurately, to the written word. So when you talk about language, the difference between understanding 50,000-80,000 words

Chapter 6

compared with the people in ancient times only having 5,000 words or less, it begins to show just one of the problems in terms of "telling."

There is a statement that goes, "I hope you understand what I mean by the words I use." A lot of times somebody says something and then you get a response back, one that clearly implied that the listener didn't understand what you meant. Then that person responds, "Yes I did understand, in fact, this is what you said" – and they will quote it. But you'll state, "Yes, but that is not what I meant." Today even the speaker, having so many choices of words, dialects, plus non-verbal body language and voice tones is often searching for ways to express himself and wants to be understood. Sometimes even the speaker is not sure that what is said is what is meant. He may also know that the listener does not necessarily understand what is meant while they are speaking. This is the problem in our complex language in the "telling model." If I tell you to sit down in your chair, that is pretty explicit. Also, if I tell you to stop because there is a car coming that maybe you haven't seen, that's again pretty explicit and pretty understandable. So there are still times where "telling" is a correct approach. However, because of the many different perceptions we have of ourselves and others, like we talked about earlier regarding emotional survival, using the "telling model" may only reach a few of the children in the classroom. This is especially true in the academic classroom if all a teacher is doing is lecturing.

It is now more productive and necessary than ever to listen, listen again, clarify the words, listen more, and clarify non-verbal themes, situational implications or statements. Restate what you are hearing, re-listen, re-clarify, and then ask for feedback to see if the speaker agrees that you have a clear understanding. Once this is accomplished, *then* the problem is solved.

In addition, we have since discovered what is called "neurolinguistics" which means language of the mind. This language takes into consideration that fact that you have five senses: sight, smell, taste, hearing, and touch. These senses are prioritized in different ways in different individuals. So just "to tell" and not use other forms of transmitting information is not going to get through to all of the students. We must develop and practice new forms of communication, enhanced ways of "telling" and explaining. This can be achieved by what is called "extra-curricular activities" as we have seen in the book, *Dead Poets*

Chapter 6

Society, a screenplay by Thomas H. Schulman, where they use experiential kinds of techniques. People who have auditory hearing strength translate things into stories. People who have visual strength translate things into pictures. People who have kinesthetic strengths translate things into forms of touch and action. Smell and taste communicate danger or pleasure, and so forth.

What we know in learning is that the more senses you can involve in any kind of learning, the quicker you learn it and the longer you remember it. So just "telling" is only part of it. Television advertisements, particularly for food, will appeal to as many senses as possible in a period of 30 to 60 seconds.

We also have another complication in the "telling" model. Telling sets up a *listen-to-tell* ear. In other words, while you are being told, you start thinking of what you are going to tell back. This goes back to the historical academic teaching model that as the teacher is talking the students are determining what to tell back. If they tell back correctly they get their "A". So what we learn from the model is that we listen to tell and don't really listen to *listen*. Then when we are told we are wrong, when we perceived that we were right ... once more the authority says "you are wrong" and punishes us instead of expounding on the response to clarify what the listener was trying to say. So there is a whole concept there that needs further understanding considering the knowledge explosion that we have. Sharing and exploring as opposed to just "telling" is one of the first things that need to change. There are many other approaches now with experiential learning.

Of course, one of the problems we have which prohibits these new approaches is in the budgeting system of our education curriculum. Programs like music, drama, art, sports, and other extra-curricular activities are the first things to be tossed out of the budget. These are extremely important in addition to the importance of knowledge in academics, technical and specific learning. Programs that include "play" (the playground) are areas in which we learn relationships, attitudes of play, survival as well as creative communication skills, etc. Budget cuts curtail the advancement of new methods of teaching, providing on-going teacher training and materials for new skills in communication. Reducing classroom size allows more time for the teacher to concentrate on each student and their learning needs. All of this is important, especially in the high-tech, emotional-survival society we live in today. The idea is that we all are in the process of *eternal* learning and what we need is understanding in all forms.

Let's go on in terms of the academic classroom. Instead of telling, we need to look in terms of sharing and relating in many forms to others, and particularly to the academic classroom. We need to use many forms to disseminate information. We must touch all senses. Today there are teaching approaches that have been developed that deal with neurolinguistics. Using these new techniques where they are applicable, plus using other new forms of learning will reach the majority of students. It has been proven that you don't even have to have small classrooms (although it helps) as long as you use this multi-approach (discussion groups, films, drama, hands-on-learning, audio programs, etc.). This total involvement in learning is what we need as opposed to just "telling."

CHAPTER 7

Add On (Batting Averages)

The second method is instead of telling you what you do wrong; change it to what I call "Batting Averages." In baseball, as an example (now played by both women and men), you work on your batting averages. Batting averages are based on 1,000. At this point no one has come close to batting a 1,000. In fact, at one time the highest season batting average in the history of baseball was 408, held by Ty Cobb. Imagine – a seasoned, famous player doesn't even hit the mark of 50%. Using this kind of measure and terminology allows you to base your educational system on "This is *what you know*--what else would you *like* to know?"

For example, look at what you know; out of ten questions you got two right. Well what can you do next time to get three or four right? Of course the old model says "You flunked, you failed", as opposed to "You got four – what can you do to get

Chapter 7

---

five or six?" So you build on "What is it that you know and what is it that you would like to know?" This is a much more positive approach versus only emphasizing what you don't know (which means you are wrong and means that you need to be punished until you are right). So think of *adding* on to what you know, by determining what else would you like or need to know.

Imagine if you were going to go to a mechanic's shop with your car. You were told this person had all kinds of technical tools, electronics and everything in this particular shop. When you arrived, you saw that there were dozens of tools all around the walls and all the latest electronic equipment. You would say that you had a basic problem with your car and would ask the mechanic for help. I think you would be quite surprised if the mechanic said, "Well, I'm not sure if I can help you. There might be one tool I don't have." Of course the person is not supposed to own every tool there is – but society says you are supposed to concentrate on what is wrong *and* to say what you don't have or know, in order to be humble. I'd probably back my car out and wonder what was wrong with that person.

There is another teaching method that uses a discovery approach. It is called the quest approach to learning and was developed by Massey Alice a professor from Harvard. This type of approach is very exciting. Kids who go to the library do all kinds of things to try to discover what it is they are trying to find. So instead of being "perfect" and "this is what it *has* to be" you change it to being efficient and effective. This approach is unique because you need to *think* when it comes to being efficient and effective as opposed to perfect.

As a young guy going through college I worked in many different areas such as plumbing, contracting, dairy work, roofing and various factory jobs. One of the factories I worked at in Indianapolis was Allison's jet plant. Of course we are talking back in 1951. At that time the jet engine was on its way to a new era. One of the things I learned was that, while a jet engine was going thousands of revolutions per second, each fin and each ball bearing and everything in that engine had to be one-thousandths of an inch to specification. If the specs were not accurate, a little wobble could cause the engine to totally fly apart. This demonstrates the level of efficiency required in order to accomplish the effect you wanted.

CHAPTER 8

Be Efficient and Effective

The Efficient/Effective method takes thinking. For example, if you took the axle on a child's wagon and you put wheels on the axle is it necessary for that axle to be one-thousandths of an inch to specification? Once moving, the delighted child might think he is going 700 miles an hour down the hill. The job only requires enough efficiency to be able to keep the wheels on so that the wagon works. If you had every axle to one-thousandths of an inch to specification, wagons would cost too much and it is not necessary. So, for efficiency's sake, you determine what it is you want your outcome to be and at what level of efficiency. Actually, that particular model can go beyond what some people think is 100%. So 100% might not be perfect, even though it is considered perfect.

Rather than the percentages, base things on what it is you are trying to accomplish. Of course, this takes *thinking*, or processing information, as opposed to being "told". You need to find the information. You might find information by someone telling you what it is, or by researching and reading about it, or by watching someone else do it. Telling, in that sense, is a part of pursuing knowledge and pursuing information.

Working and thinking about being efficient and effective is the third method. This creates the question "What am I trying to accomplish and what level of efficiency do I choose?" You go through those stages of determining with the students what they need to learn and what knowledge is already there. Use many forms of sharing to get people excited about learning. Instead of saying, "You didn't know this" try, "Well you know this much, what else might you need to know." This is a more "effective" and a constructive method. This allows you to learn something new and go on!

CHAPTER 9

Be Response- "Able"

Be responsible! You are supposed to do what the authority says. This is very interesting because one of the problems we have, just like the language explosion, and the knowledge explosion, is that we now have many, many authorities.

Years ago in a small town, even today in some of the smaller towns; they had few basic laws to live by. Of course there were some criminal laws, social laws, family/marital laws, traffic laws, etc. In essence, you had a basic set of social values. I grew up in a small town of 5,000 people in Indiana – everybody knew that the factories got out at 5:00 p.m. and that everybody ate at 5:30 so all the kids were sent home at 5:30 because that is when everybody had supper. Everybody knew their neighbors and knew where they were. In fact, as boys we were told that we were supposed to stay away from "old Joe" (as an example) because old Joe would tell you things you weren't supposed to

Chapter 9

know. (Of course all it did was encourage us boys to go look up old Joe to find out these things. That is how we got our education in those *other* areas of learning that we "weren't supposed to know" about.) Anyway, that aside, back then you had basic laws, a basic set of religious systems – maybe two to three churches in a town. So if you didn't know what to do you could turn to any one of those authorities and follow any one of them and you would be a "responsible" person. (The established guidelines were the law, social values, trusted neighbors, and your church). So back then you could do what you should do and if you did what you should do according to one of those authorities, then you were accepted, responsible, and acknowledged as someone who was contributing.

Now, there's a problem, how many churches or religions do we have in cities today? Even within the Christian faith how many translations of the scriptures do we now have? How many spiritual or religious authorities do we have? There is everything from Krishna, Islam, Hindu, to many forms of Christianity, to Judaism, to various other protestant denominations, new age, to name a few. We have all forms of religious systems prevalent just in America. Each tells us what we should do in order to be responsible. Take a look at law, such as library law, corporate law, divorce law, palimony law, space law, environmental law, intellectual law, etc. Even lawyers within their own fields disagree with each other. But again you are supposed to know what you should do and must be responsible.

In regard to social values, half the time I don't even know my next door neighbors, let alone what they believe, but we are supposed to follow the basic social values. Look at how much information is provided (think about the vast information and "authorities" that are available on the internet). Even the media has become an "authority" by presenting what is perceived to be "politically correct." Responsibility is to do, to act, and to believe the way one "*should.*" This, of course, is governed by religious, legal, social, and institutional (educational) authorities.

Today, to question the "authority" is not acceptable. In our educational system, questioning the authority as a student means that you might be sent to the principal's office or experiencing your parents being required to come to school for a parent-teacher conference. It is basically a fact that teachers and schools are RIGHT and students and parents are mostly WRONG. This is an essential principle in the educational system today.

Chapter 9

All of this is quite a problem. One day as I was reading David W. Augsburger's book, *Caring Enough to Confront* (Regal Books), I read his comment about having the *ability* to *respond* in life. That really set off a revelation and a new idea in my head. This idea was that your basic authority is *life itself*. Of course life itself would be your *mental* life (knowledge base), your *emotional* life, your *social/cultural* life (which includes your family), and your *physical* life (your body, your whole being, as well as your physical environment). All of these resources are then connected and led by your *spiritual* life.

"With these five resources and five intelligences we are each a universe with endless potential."

George Rosselot

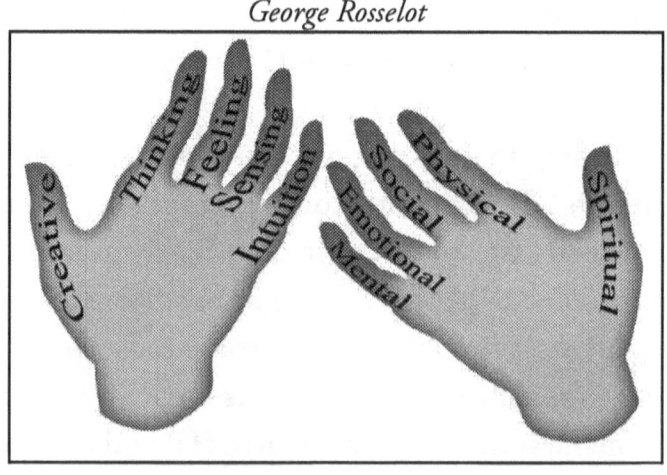

"It's all in your hands!"
Our Five Resources ~ Our Five Intelligences

Take a look at your hand with the palm of your hand facing you. Each finger can be a symbol for one of the first four resources listed above. Plus your thumb represents your spiritual life. You literally hold your five resources in your hand with your spiritual resource leading, able to touch and connect the other four. In addition, your other hand represents the five intelligences of your life. They are intuition (knowing), sensing (action), feeling (joy, sadness, warmth), and thinking (logic) with the last being creativity. Again, like the spiritual resource, the thumb represents the creative intelligence. It is able to touch and connect to the other four.

Preservation of life is "the basic authority." These five resources and five intelligences of a human being must be preserved. So whatever is done needs to be done to preserve life. This means that I can *consider* any of the dozens of authorities as long as the basic factor is to preserve life.

In addition to this preservation, you must set up the ability to respond. Note that a response predicts the next response and that one predicts the next ability to respond, and so forth. You now have the insight of response-ability vs. responsibility. This innovative process sets up the ability to respond and to negotiate responsibly – then I can do it. But if it does not set up response-"able"ness then I would not do it. The new definition of responsibility is response-ability. The goal is to act and internalize beliefs that assure my own and other(s) ability to respond now and in future "nows."

Being responsible (or response-"able") in a complex society	
Responsibility	**Respons(e)-Ability**
Definition: To do, to act, and to believe the way one "should."	Definition: To act and internalize beliefs that assures my own and others "ability to respond now and in future nows."
AUTHORITIES Religious Legal Social Values	**AUTHORITIES** Preservation of life – "being-ness and existence" of living things and support systems of life forms.
To obey and abide by one or all three of these is to be responsible.	To preserve and add on to life and support systems to life (mine and others), to assure the ability to respond, respond and respond now and in future nows is to be response-"able".

CHAPTER 10

The Actualization of What You Know

Just one thing ... what happened to humility? In this new idea – the more you know the more there is to know and you find out how exciting life can be – you look at these five methods in Emotional Survival and you notice that there is no punishment model. There are natural consequences in terms of something that didn't work because you didn't know something. As Adler says, a mistake is a misdirected action because of something you didn't know. So the idea is to know, to learn and to cooperate with each other in all forms.

The alternative is I am always going to be told that I am wrong or I have to watch out for being wrong or somebody is going to tell me I am wrong. The current "humility model" states the more you know the more you find out the less you know. The implication is that if you take on

Chapter 10

---

an attitude that you are "all knowing" you will be egotistical or have a swelled head or worse-case scenario perceive that you are "God"! It is important to realize that we are small and insignificant and really less-than compared to the universe and creation itself. We are going to take a position, if you are going to take it to extremes, of "I've got to know everything to be able to point out that I am not wrong and point out that everybody else is wrong" – or I take the position of being upset and angry because I am getting tired of being told I am wrong. Therefore I am not going to pay any attention to what anybody says and I am going to go off on my own.

We use all kinds of words like passive resistance and passive aggression because basically we are tired of being told we are wrong and we are tired of being told that we somehow have to be humble and we have to be sure we don't expound how much we do know. Even the little things are supposed to be noticed, admonished, and corrected.

One of the things I found out in terms of human actualization training is you get a group of people in the room. The first thing you ask them to do is take their paper and pencil and write down 50 things that they know are really good

The Actualization of What You Know

about themselves. The people just look at you sort of stymied. They can write 50 things that they know they don't know, or they can write what about where they are wrong. They can easily pick apart all the bad elements of themselves. But how many times does anyone ask you to write or (heaven forbid) say 50 wonderful or good things about yourself – or what you like about yourself. This whole emphasis is the opposite of looking at what you don't know and looking at what is wrong. Again, the more you know, the more you find out the less you know. This is part of that humility myth. And I call it a myth.

So let's take this new approach, the more you know, the more you find out there is more to know...*how exciting life can be!* A very good friend of mine is Dr. Shapiro. He is a psychiatrist in Akron, Ohio. We worked together while I was guidance director of a public high school in nearby Hudson, Ohio. He taught me a very interesting concept relating to humility. It goes like this:

<u>**Scenario #1**</u> - A party is going on and a person pulls up in his van and he unloads his electric guitar and speakers, knocks on the door and says he has arrived and walks on in. People buzz around and ask, "Who is this? Has

Chapter 10

anybody engaged a band or music, or special entertainment?" to which everyone says no. The guy is all set up now and he plays. And he is excellent. The people really enjoy it and they start to clap. Surprisingly he says, "No, do not clap now. I will tell you when to applaud because that is how good I am."

Scenario #2 - Again a party is going on and it is getting kind of dull and someone understands that a certain person at the party plays a guitar. The person says, "Look, how about livening up the party a little and playing for us." The guitar player says, "Well I didn't know in advance and I don't have my guitar." So the person replies "Someone in this house just got a brand new guitar. Would you try it?" So he says he will try. He gets a guitar and he tunes it to be sure it is perfectly tuned and then he says, "Well I think I have a couple songs I've practiced well enough that I could play for you." So he plays his few songs and he is also excellent! The people say how wonderful he is, that he is a great guitar player but the guitar player says, "Well, if I had known in advance, I probably could have been better. And if I'd had a little more time to practice the ones that I did play I probably could have played better – but oh well, OK, thanks anyway."

Scenario #3 - A similar situation of a party is going on. The party begins to get dull and someone says to the new guy, "We hear you play the guitar." He agrees that he does. "How about playing for us", they ask. "Well I don't have my guitar", he responds. The guy in the house brings out his brand new guitar and asks, "How about it?" The new guy says he'll play. He takes the guitar, he tunes it up and he says, "OK, call out some songs." They call out some songs and he plays the ones he knows and he is excellent and they have a great time. When it is all over they remark to the guitar player how wonderful it was and how well he played. He responds, "I sure appreciated your asking me and I was honored and glad to play. I had a great time, too."

Now, which one of these three people in these scenarios do we say is humble? Most of us would say the 2nd person is most humble because he is not interested in saying how good he is and he back-steps and could be better. That is how we are taught – you are not *supposed* to say how good you are. But essentially he is the *least* humble of the three. The first person is obviously arrogant and egotistical. However, an example of an egotist would be someone who says, if I learn something I'll be better than anyone else so I'm not going to

Chapter 10

learn it because if I did I'd put everybody to shame. That's an egotist, someone who sits back and says what they *can* do but half the time they can't do what they even say they can do. No, instead this first guy is arrogant and eccentric. He is good, he knows he is good, and he tells everyone he is good. That is an eccentric. They are kind of hard to get along with though in certain situations they are excellent at what they share with us. But in some cases we are willing to accept their excellence and eccentricities because they are so good.

It was the person in the third scenario that is probably the most humble. He is willing to own, he is willing to share, and willing to acknowledge his talents by sincerely expressing his appreciation and thanks.

This is what Dr. Shapiro shared to illustrate these three stages and to explain the true meaning of humility. I wanted to share this with you because I think that we have been taught the second approach where we are supposed to apologize because we could have been better – back to "the more I know the less I know," compared to the more I know the more I know there is more to contribute which is really the true sense of humility.

The Actualization of What You Know

Again we can go back to love thy neighbor as thyself. The more you know of yourself the more you add on to yourself and the more you have to contribute to others. I like to think of it as each person is like a flowing spring.

In Tallahassee, Florida we have Wakulla Springs, and in Indiana there is Wawasee Springs where thousands of gallons of spring water flow out from the earth. People would stop and get a drink and be refreshed. So think of it as a constantly flowing spring, the more you add-on the more you have to give. Like the natural spring, it flows on down the aquifer. The fish, the green ferns, the little animals and the deer, not to mention the joy of human beings canoeing down the stream contribute to life itself. So when I add on to my life, am my own best friend, (which might be another way of saying love thy neighbor as thyself) I am splashing out into other peoples' buckets. It is self-ness. Eric Fromm talks about self-ness, which is the willingness to add on and then to give. Adding-on, in order to give, is being unselfish.

This is the opposite of being dipped out of (rather than over-flowing), like the old farm pump where eventually it loses its prime where you then have to pour more water into it to get it going

Chapter 10

again. If I let myself be dipped-out and dipped-out until there is nothing left to give, essentially that looks like I'm being unselfish and humble yet at the same time, I'd be limiting myself from being able to contribute. To go even further, if I add-on and then put a lid on it, it is greed and selfishness.

We must be willing to add-on. As Adler again said – when I act out of my own best interest I pave the way for others to develop their own best interest. I have noticed that acting out of your own best interest is sometimes seen as being selfish. However, when you act in your own best interest, as your own best friend, loving others as you love yourself, you pave the way for other people to act out of their own best interest and to be their own best friend. This adding on creates an overflow that contributes to others.

A good example is Dorothy Hammel. She won the Olympic gold metal in ice-skating; she acknowledged that she had won and that it was a wonderful moment. She was acknowledging her accomplishment. You *can* own it; it is wonderful to learn, to add-on and to share. That is really humility in its best sense. Even Christ, in His humility, owned who He was and what He had to contribute which was being humble and He continually added on. Like an Eternal Spring, His splashing out throughout history gave us love and sharing which influenced others to add on to their lives to then contribute to the rest of us.

SECTION III

Guideline for Maintaining a Firm Footing in a World Where Change is Constant

Concept: Change is constant. However, you can produce security within insecurity by the following "thinking" and "acting" steps.

Guideline for Maintaining a Firm Footing in a World Where Change is Constant

Step 1

In light of present knowledge:

a. Act, or

b. Sometimes "act not to act" due to insufficient knowledge or insight. This *is* a decision.

Step 2

In light of new (or present) knowledge I can move beyond past decisions or actions staying on the cutting edge or "now" time (present toward future). *New* knowledge or insight creates a *new* situation, such as:

a. Obtaining or introducing new knowledge or new insights creates a new decision to be made. The result is that the first decision can be disregarded, altered or reaffirmed.

b. The slightest new insight, knowledge or situational change can create a new decision *option*. "Saving face" now occurs as all involved win at an increased level *without* rejecting the other person or self. Appropriateness is achieved by using the criteria of response-"able"ness. The new information may affirm to keep the previous decision which then essentially becomes new based on new information. You are, therefore, always operating on what is new.

c. A cooperation model to create new knowledge, insight or situation *enhances* human relationships. We become problem solvers and explorers with others and ourselves.

In human relationships, cooperation, rather than competition is more likely to produce constructive outcomes and results. Outcomes such as caring for each other, using the team approach, sharing, friendship, intimacy, trust and openness are realized to a fuller extent. However, to compete is to be involved with one-upmanship – good/bad – right/wrong polarities. When relationship is the goal, competition becomes counterproductive because if you win you lose and if you lose you lose.

Using the concept of "in light of present knowledge" the following chapters will provide principles and ideas that will further enhance and affirm who you are as an individual and how you relate to others.

CHAPTER 11

Fair-Mindedness and Equality

Nothing in life is fair, but we can be fair-minded and work toward a "something for something" outcome. Correspondingly, nothing in life is equal, but we can have equal respect for each other.

We've been taught that nothing in life is fair. Therefore in a lot of current thought people say, "Well, I make up my own rules and what I want to do, and therefore I get to do whatever I want to do and that's what's fair. It has to be my way." More appropriately, we can work toward being fair-minded. So fair-minded is like following the <u>rules, roles, and boundaries</u> *(see Appendix C)* in terms of how you are fair-minded and how you play fair. So one of the things we review is what the understandings are, what are the rules, and who does what – what are the roles, what are the

Chapter 11

---

boundaries, what is the time line we are working on? And it is like checkers, we know what the rules, roles and boundaries are, or chess or cards, or volleyball, or kickball, or skip rope, all kinds of things – dozens and dozens. Each one is identified because of its rules, roles and boundaries and then we do everything to follow those rules, roles and boundaries and play fair. Be fair-minded in what we do.

When people set up the rules, roles and boundaries, and have understandings to which they agree, then people follow these and people say you are playing fair. In playing fair you also "stay in there". So fair-minded is to be willing to follow what is agreed upon and then be fair-minded in how we operate. The interesting thing here is play, or let's say the playground of whatever it is we play, is where we learn our interpersonal relationships. The play area, or how we played, is basically how we have developed our interpersonal relationships.

In education, things that we consider play like extracurricular activities, athletics, music or drama are where we really learn the interaction among and between us as human beings.

The following chart provides examples of two kinds of kids:

Productive	Destructive
Creative	Bully
Shares	Know-it-all
Organizer	Cheat
Encourager	Changes rules for own benefit
Owns mistakes	Not dependable
Team player	Disloyal
Sets up equipment	Take "my" ball and go home
Includes others	Blames
Takes lead and can follow	Complains
Problem solver	Temper/Fight to get own way
Loyal	Tease
Mediator	Tattler
Seeks out authorities in a non-tattle way	Show off
Plays hard	Prima Donna
Kind	Mean

Chapter 11

The *productive* group follows the rules, roles and boundaries and plays fair. They hang in there and they have respect for what they are doing and for each other. The *destructive* group disregards rules, roles and boundaries and is essentially selfish and self-centered.

We've also experienced that nothing in life is equal. So the attitude can be that I can do what I want to do because nothing is equal anyway. It is up to me to decide what I choose to do and what I think I want. Some people are tall, some are older, and some people have skills that are different than other people. For example, take somebody six foot six and someone else five foot eight – if we're watching a ball game through a fence the taller person can look over the fence and see the whole game and the shorter person has to look through an eye hole.

However, we can work toward equal respect which gives each of us ability to respond. This is enhanced by using the first three concepts: to have response"able"ness, to preserve life and to be fair-minded as well as have equal respect. This again goes back to rules, roles and boundaries to where we play fair and we have respect for each other and for what we are doing. We can work together with insight and understanding. We're working together using those other two concepts that we first started with to have ability to respond. We have equal respect with whomever we are playing and dealing.

CHAPTER 12

Life is Made for Me

Instead: Life is here to be dealt with – but in a kind, firm, understanding and caring way – a lifetime process of growth.

Well, that's a wonderful thought and we would hope that life would be there for you in positive ways. One of the problems with "life is supposed to be made for me" is that if that were really true then I would have to follow what someone else set up for me to do. That means life is made for me, do what is set up for me to do, and it is all laid out for me and that is the way it is. The book, *I Never Promised You a Rose Garden*, by Joanne Greenberg (Penguin Books), is where a little girl believed that concept and found out the real world wasn't that way. She therefore went into a fantasy world because she found out doing everything right didn't necessarily mean that life would be made for her.

Chapter 12

The bottom line is life is not made for me. Life is here to deal with. That means I have a choice. That gives the inference that I have the ability to deal with and work with life and to work through life and to negotiate life.

In reviewing these concepts, I want to preserve life in every way, I want to be fair-minded, I want to have equal respect, and I want to be able to deal with life in a way that provides response-ability. To deal with life, after we've gone through those steps is to work toward win-win.

CHAPTER 13

Win-Win

The goal: Work toward a win-win with self and others.

Covey in his works talks about win-win. In working through life with these steps, work toward a win-win is where we can negotiate in such a way that there is something fair when I negotiate with someone else. So that doesn't mean it would be two for you, two for me, two for you, two for me, like one of the cartoons of Donald Duck. Donald was issuing different kinds of goodies, and then he would say one for Huey, one for Donald, one for Dewey, one for Donald, and one for Luey and one for Donald. The three boys were sort of puzzled and couldn't figure out what was going on. That's not a win-win. In win-win always regard preservation of life, be fair-minded, have equal

Chapter 13

respect, and willingness to deal with the situation toward negotiation. These are the initial concepts toward living creatively, courageously, and supporting the concept that good guys can be gutsy.

In a win-win situation, it is saying "I will do everything in my power not to hurt you. Likewise, neither will I allow you to knowingly or inadvertently hurt me. Were I to let you hurt me it would not be fair to you since you would not have the best of me to enjoy." Be able to stand firm and say "As long as it is a win-win and we follow these fair-minded concepts, I am willing to negotiate, otherwise I am not."

When you are talking about fair-mindedness and win-win, as long as a person is willing to accept these concepts/steps, be fair-minded, set up an ability to respond, and have equal respect where we have the best interest, both of the community as well as each other, then you have a negotiating basis for whatever you negotiate. Sometimes something for something can be five for you, three for me; six for me, four for you, and is based on the fact the people are using these given concepts in order to make any kind of decision or to work through any issues on which they have differences.

There is another element that is added to this principle – the teachings of "turning the other cheek" and "forgive seventy times seven." In today's more abusive society it is important to add on to this teaching by saying "Hit me once and you've got my attention. I'm willing to deal with you in a fair-minded way, but you are not going to hit me again." It is based on the concept that though I care for you, it is not appropriate for me to allow you to hurt me or allow you to hurt another living being because life is precious. These concepts are somewhat different than what we normally hear. You are still being kind and caring, but you can stand firm on the concept of working towards win-win.

CHAPTER 14

The Spiral of Vulnerability

This is a very interesting concept. This illustrates what is needed in determining honesty levels, openness, decision-making and behavior.

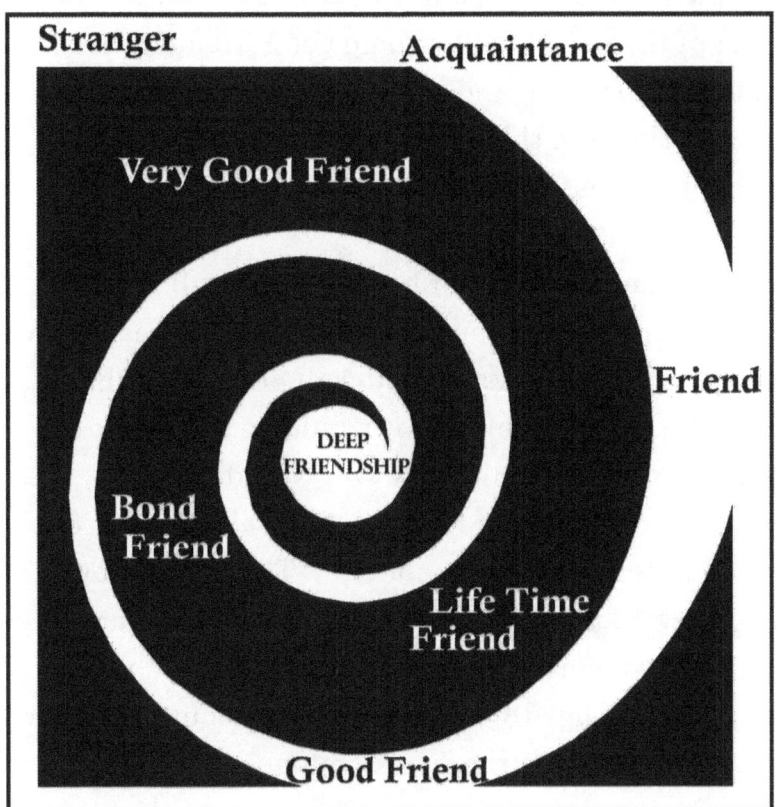

Chapter 14

You meet a stranger, they ask "What's your name, where do you live, what to you do for a living, what is your phone number" ... it is like saying, "Excuse me but I don't know who you are. Do you have credentials or are you a figure of authority?" In some situations you may even have to contact your attorney before you will answer certain questions. So for a stranger you may be honest and say you don't know that person and are not willing to answer the questions. Then strangers can become acquaintances, who then can become friends, and as you go down through the internal part of the spiral you become good friends, then very good friends and possibly bonded friends. As you go through this spiral you may go into these deeper stages.

The first is, I am honest and I will honestly share things with you, I am not going to lie. I may say "Sorry I don't know you well enough to share that with you" ... even if it would be a positive answer. I don't know how you would use the answer. The person might say, "Well you just don't want to tell me." True enough. There are some people who move on down into that spiral and they tell everyone all about themselves and then they realize they hardly know anything about the other person. They are then very vulnerable.

The Spiral of Vulnerability

When people are moving in together, in terms of sharing knowledge, sharing life and sharing personal information, one person may be sharing more than the other and vice versa. Eventually you may reach a level in which you can trust that other person – particularly with personal and private information. An example of an honesty level would be, "I will be honest with you and will not lie to you. However, I am not willing to let you know everything, because honesty is a like a court of law – you've got to ask me the right question. I don't know you well enough and I don't honestly know what your motives are." It is basically saying that if I understand what the motives are, positive or not, I'd be glad to consider answering – but otherwise in honesty, I can say that I am not willing to answer.

On the other hand, if I really know other people, I know I can be open and share anything that they are not even aware of. This is because I trust and know their beliefs and I trust that they will be able to handle something very difficult and that we'll work through it as two people that have become deep, bonded friends. Even in the most difficult situation I know the person will work with me to achieve understandings and resolve whatever difficulties or traumas that might exist.

Chapter 14

Ultimately, you will be able to move into the part of the spiral where knowing each other and understanding each others' values and considering the well-being of each other will take place. This still uses the central theme of the preservation of life and working toward the well-being of the community and each other, in every way possible.

I think one of the biggest issues is the need to negotiate what would be in everyone's best interest. Even in the best interest of who we perceive to be our enemies we should pursue what would help them as well as help us in making us OK with each other and the situation. You present terms where everyone has a benefit. Again, it doesn't have to be equal; it can be fair-minded with equal respect to where we achieve the best possible outcomes. All of this involves mental, emotional, social, cultural, physical, spiritual and cosmic elements.

Courageous and creative people can stand up and at times be willing to deal with difficult situations. One must work toward best interests; work with these tools and concepts. These tools and the tool of reflective (active) listening *(see Appendix A)* will help work toward insight and understanding. These are the tools and concepts that need to be taught – many of which are not being taught today! These are the things we need to know and put into action at a very early age!

CHAPTER 15

Take Charge!

Take Charge – You're a Miracle!

This can be the way you negotiate with yourself in terms of am I being my own best friend or am I being fair-minded. Follow those steps in terms of dealing with life and best interest of your own development, and your own self-growth. This gets into many areas one of which is we're taught that we're supposed to be in control. Always be in control and stay in control. Another way of looking at control is thinking of it in terms of *"taking charge."*

Whenever someone claims they have to exert self-control, change it immediately to taking charge. I like the idea that if you are trying to take on something new, let whatever caused the problem be the reminder to change it. So if you hear yourself say "should" change it to *"would"* you

Chapter 15

be willing. When I hear myself say that I must be in control the phrase would be more positive and powerful if changed to "I choose to take charge."

This in a sense is an additional concept. There are many more. So the big question is what am I in charge of? Well, bottom line, I am in charge of myself. What am I? What's my gender, what's my nationality, how am I defined? Basically there are four steps to self-concept. What I actually am, what I think myself to be, what I think others perceive me to be, and what other people tell me I am. So what I am, my genetics, my gender, my social-cultural situation and what I think myself to be is based on all kinds of things from my interpretation of myself and other people's interpretation. Then I interpret myself as this is who I am and look to others to see if they validate that.

One important thing is I need to look at *significant* others not just "generalized others." There are *significant others* that are willing to be objective in terms of validating what and who I am. Sometimes other people want to tell me what they think I ought to be or what they think I ought to be for them, and many times this gets into wanting to run me or control me or possibly even put me down.

Or, to the opposite end, telling me that I am this fantastic great individual that ought to be a great athlete or musician, etc. I need to find significant others, people that are objective to validate what I see myself to be. If those things fit what I really I can get to the first steps of self-concept.

Back to taking charge, I am really looking at what I am. Basically, I AM A MIRACLE. As a miracle I am very precious. It's like being more precious than any rare jewels or rare objects. I am one of a kind. Fingerprints may not always be accurate, now DNA is a more accurate way to define a specific individual. So we have progressed in many ways in terms of the fact that we are miracles and we perform miracles.

Using the basic concept that our Maker created a human being in His own image, means that He created a being exactly like Him with the same potential that He has. Now that sounds rather strange because as far as we know the Word was with God, the Word said let there be Light, let there be the Heavens, and "Let there be..." and it happened. Well, unfortunately at this point, I don't know too many people that can say "Let there be" and speak a word in that context and it happens. Such as let there be a cure for cancer, let there be

Chapter 15

a million dollars in my pocket, let there be... It is almost like the idea that God put here, all of His abilities, wisdom, intelligence and creativity. But in His wisdom, He wants us to discover it so that we have the same joy that He had when creating what He created. We are basically miracles and we've been put in the position that everything is here for us to discover and explore. Hopefully we just described a way of being courageous, using those steps in exploring and negotiating with ourselves and with other people.

Let's look at areas in terms of being a miracle:

- The human race has always been in awe as to what the human being can produce. For example, the bow and arrow, fire, the printing press, large ships and all of the inventions, even more so as technology came along. Around the end of World War II and maybe even beginning before that there were some people that started looking at the human being as one of the most marvelous engineering feats to ever be discovered. The physical miracle of cybernetics is really the human being. The study of the human brain is still being done to discover all that we know in developing computers, etc. We still haven't found a computer that thinks for itself even though we are working on artificial intelligence. The problem with computers is who is going to put the values and belief systems into that computer. Of course, we have all kinds of science fiction that deals with that. All of our computers and systems are designed after the neuron-system of the brain.

- Sound systems study the human ear and voice box in terms of how the sounds are produced and how the sounds are received. Amazingly, within the ear's sound systems are two little bones that are phenomenal in how they work and how they differentiate different kinds of sound to where we understand language and we understand tones and so forth.

- The cranes and lifting systems are all designed after the human muscle and joint systems. We automatically reach out and pick something up. Orthopedic inventions designed for the human body relate to how much stress and tension are needed and are all extremely refined in terms of the human body. In bending over and picking

Chapter 15

up something, engineers study the joint and musculature system for developing lifting devices. The more complex the lifting devices, the more sophisticated the computer that is running it.

- The nervous system is very interesting because the nerves sense when touched by something and our mind immediately knows where it was touched and if it were comfortable or uncomfortable, itchy or whatever. So the human nerve system is studied in terms of communication fiber optics, for example. The fiber in fiber optic looks like a little fishing line which looks like a human nerve and from what I understand, fiber can transmit 1,500 to 2,000 messages at one time through the transmission of light. If you have one cable with 24 fibers in it, just think of how many thousands of messages are going across with one cable. The system that developed fiber optics included studying the human nerve system and being intrigued by how a human nerve can transmit as fast and rapidly the many messages that it can all at one time. The more technical the machine the more it is designed after the human body.

- Another example is the heart; it seems to be the most efficient, effective pump in terms of how it operates. Think about the functioning of the heart and how it continuously beats and the transportation systems of your veins and arteries and how the valve systems work and how flexible they all are – especially in space where the body contracts or expands. The human veins, artery, heart and valve systems are all studied in terms of how they work. We're getting down to high tech valve systems in many areas.

- The human skin is very fascinating. Old skin sheds off and new skin is grown. To my understanding, on the first space capsule the heat shield was not one solid piece of metal or wood (which would heat up and burn). It was made of layers and layers of materials that can come back through the atmosphere and peel off and still protect the astronauts. That was designed after the human skin. The human skin is very flexible and stretches. The human skin is studied.

- Inside a person's mouth – your cellular system completely replaces itself and those cells are studied. For example, if tires have

Chapter 15

a leak, the material placed inside the tire automatically seals the leak. In the mouth, if you bite yourself, the tissue replaces itself with no scar.

- Of course we still don't have a machine that gives birth – but we must include the miracle of birth and reproduction. Industrialization and assembly lines that reproduce items may appear that way but to date a machine cannot initially reproduce itself.

The *real* miracle is a human being. The above only discusses the physical self. YOU ARE A MIRACLE. In addition, think of the ability to gain knowledge and other resources, your emotions, your social/cultural and your spiritual areas. These major resources are huge miracles. Consider that we have five resources: Thinking, Sensing, Intuition, Feeling, and Creative.

Consider the intriguing aspect of intuition. Interestingly, Judith Farina, an instructor at the University of Connecticut at Stamford contends that "intuitive feelings are based on past experiences we cannot immediately recall." Dr. Weston H. Agor, a political scientist and psychologist at the University of Texas at El

Paso who is the author of *Intuitive Management* (Prentice-Hall) also believes that intuition has a solid rational basis. It is highly biological. He says, "Our body has been assimilating cues and is now retrieving the relevant information for us automatically."

Men call intuition a gut feeling or a hunch. Women are now starting to use the words gut feeling. Intuition essentially is the most complex of these five resources. You get a read on something on which you pick up and then you use the other resources to determine as to what you actually picked up. There has been a lot of research in terms of intuition. It seems that the more life experiences and successful ways that things work out positively, the greater one can trust intuition. Believing intuition is strictly based on nothing but feeling is one little part of it. Add the fact that there is a primary rationale and determine where the action formation is as well as feeling and you see where your intuition is coming from.

One thing that my wife has is very keen intuition. Over the 30 plus years that we have worked in our clinic together, about five times she has come to me before I see a new person and said "I need to see you." I asked what's up and she said

Chapter 15

things like "little hairs on the back of my neck are standing up." Every single time, the person was a high-risk person – potentially dangerous. So talk about intuition, thank goodness it has only been about five times in 30 years that her intuition denoted danger. There is intuition and it is more than just "woman's intuition." Intuition is just a primary part of the five resources we, as miracle creations, possess.

It seems that human beings seem to be connected at a deep level. James Allen, in his book *As a Man Thinketh*, states that as we influence each other and as we think in positive ways we influence the world and it is a realm where there is no language barrier. Thinking in positive ways and thinking in creative ways goes into the universal collective unconscious or intuition or prayer, and so forth. So bottom line human beings, male and female, acquire and develop all five resources. We are a creative, sensing, thinking, feeling, and intuitive human miracle!

Take Charge – Know How You Affect Others

We have five intelligences and five resources. There is another illustration I share in terms of being a miracle. Each of us is a country. Each person is in charge of one's own country, negotiating with other people as countries. The idea of country is quite amazing and can be spread in many different directions, blending our differences and similarities. Interesting – in communication, we use four communication channels: <u>what I say</u>, <u>what I hear</u>, <u>what the other person says</u>, <u>what the other person hears</u>. With three people, you square it to 9, with four people there are 16, with five people there are 25 communication factors going on in that group.

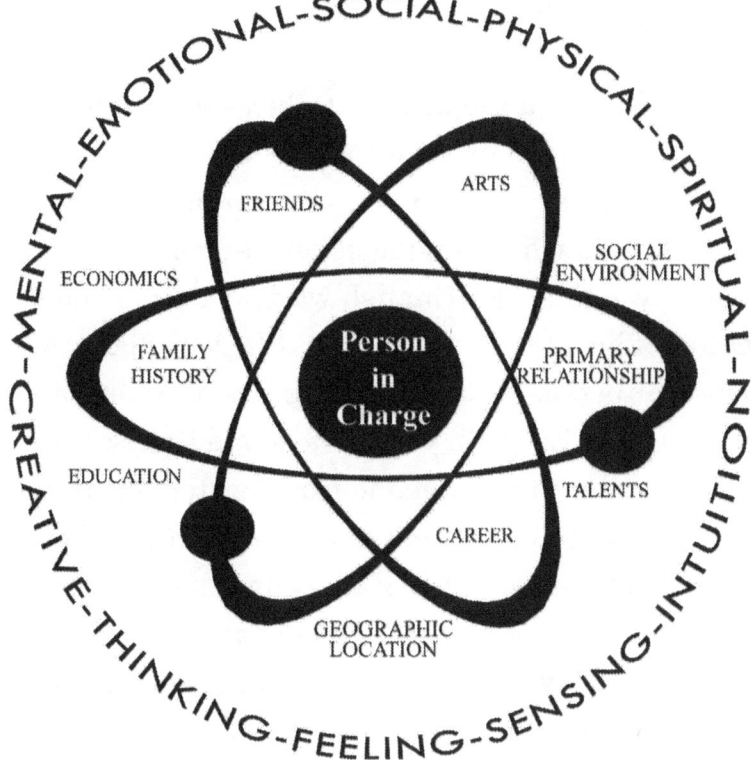

Chapter 15

You, as a country, co-exist with other countries. It is almost like an airport traffic controller directing the central station, tarmacs and all the different planes taking off. Each one interrelates and affects the other so whatever you do, you need the controller to be able to organize and make sure these things work together. So when you talk about each person as a country, with its own language, its own non-verbal language, its own perception and intuitions and feelings, and its own way of seeing itself when you are with another individual – it is like working toward blending countries and all of the variances and intricacies.

When you see different places or different situations as a country, we are talking about what language do we speak, what non-verbal language do we speak, what languages do we know, even though we all speak English we may come from many different territories with different dialects. Consider people from different parts of America, we all speak English, yet at the same time we have different dialects. Someone from Boston speaking to someone from out west may misinterpreted or not be understood. One of the words used in the south was a standard greeting of "hey" and I would reply "hi." Hey (hay) was something that was in a field. High is something up in the air.

When you think of all of this, plus all the differences and subtleties we and add in the dynamic emotional survival issues, where even our unconscious plays a role, it is amazing that we are able to communicate and comprehend each other at all! When you think in terms of how complex each person is, and how we interact, it is profound. We must work toward the best interest of everyone, each must be courageous and it takes using these concepts we've talked about, like friendship and working together. In that sense we are joining a team of courageous people and working toward each person's best interest while being kind, firm, understanding, and caring for others as well as ourselves.

So what do you do with the miracle? Discard it? Let it be stomped over? Not acknowledge it? No, I think when you realize you are a miracle, even if you begin with just the physical miracle of what we are you think, how do I want to take charge of it? You begin to use these concepts in terms of taking charge and negotiating.

Chapter 15

Take Charge – Good Guys Can Be Gutsy

Some people think only of themselves. Alternatively, consider the following:

In win-win it is saying "I will do everything in my power not to hurt you. Likewise, neither will I allow you to hurt me knowingly or inadvertently. Were I to let you hurt me it would not be FAIR to YOU since you would NOT have the best ME to ENJOY."

This statement is used when you're dealing with somebody who won't accept or understand these creative, constructive concepts. You must be able to say to that person, I care about you, or love you (or both), and I will not let you hurt me even unintentionally, definitely not intentionally. Because if I let you hurt me, even unintentionally, then I am not going to be the interesting, creative person that I am capable of being, and that's not fair to you. I'll do my best not to hurt you, but you need to know that I will do everything to preserve life. If you are in the mode of destroying life, you might be faced with a formidable foe. I will not permit you to hurt me and I will support life. So if you want to negotiate using fair-minded, equal respect, preservation of life and response-ableness, there is a win-win. If not, then what I understand is that you don't understand and I'm not willing to go there. There are ways that I can share what I think will be fair for both of us. And if you can come up with ideas that will be positive, ideas for you and me, I'll be glad to consider them.

I had an experience years ago in a business. I was supportive of one of my partners who consistently misused the office resources such as having the secretaries take his car to the shop and run personal errands for him. These were definitely not business responsibilities and not for what we were paying our secretaries. At one point, being rather concerned about all of this, I consulted an attorney friend of mine who indicated that I was being too nice. Of course I asked him to explain what he meant by "too nice." He said, well you are always giving in.

At that point I realized it was not appropriate for me to allow my business partner to upset or use me. Again, if you'll negotiate with me on a win-win, fine – otherwise, I will work with you seventy-times seven toward a positive outcome. So in negotiating with my business partner I bought him

Chapter 15

out and made sure that the on-going business and staff was fine and appropriate business procedures were restored.

Another term is forgiveness. People think of forgiveness as "I forgive you." Many times we say I forgive you, and we assume that it is the other person's immediate responsibility to let go of everything. Let's break down the word: forgive. I am *for* – and I am willing to *give* the energy and resources it takes to resolve whatever the issues are. So I will forgive, I will *give* seventy-times seven the energy to resolve those issues toward our best interest for the preservation of life. This encompasses all the things we've talked about and I will work with you, with anyone, toward that best interest. This is also in the best interest of community and society. I think that these concepts are somewhat different than we normally hear. You are still being kind and caring, but you stand firm on the concepts of working toward win-win.

Carl Adler said, "To work toward one's own best interest is to pave the way for other people toward their best interest." Best interest today may be misinterpreted as selfish interest. So I restate ... working toward one's own best interest as one's own best friend paves the way for other people to work toward their best interest and be their own best friend. This brings up the subject of friendship.

Friendship is one of the major keys I've shared in relation to the Red Pencil. Friendship has within it the characteristics of a courageous person using rules, roles and boundaries, and playing fair, understanding each other with equal respect and working toward best outcome. This is working toward the best interest of creative, positive friends.

This brings up another concept and that is what Adler talked about: *taking sails down*. He got this idea from looking at the tall ships years ago. The historical tall ships had huge sails. Some of them were five masts and some of them were three. If you take a ship, the tallest pole, or mast to hold the sails, would be shored up at the top of the ship and go all the way to the bottom of the ship which would be the keel. The shorter masts, which would be built and shored up at the top, would not have to go all the way to the bottom of the ship. In a storm, the sailors would rapidly have to take down the center mast sails and if they couldn't get the center mast's sail down fast enough they would chop the center mast down. Because

Chapter 15

---

if they weren't able to do either then the center mast's pressure would split open the bottom of the boat. So one of the things that Adler came up with, in any kind of conflict, is do your best to take the sails down. We've been taught to take the wind out of somebody's sails, but he is talking about taking the sails out of the person's wind. That way the possibility of being able "to stay afloat" or to deal with the situation can take place constructively.

Taking the wind out of the person's sails is a power play. In a sailing race, if you are going to try to overcome another sail boat, you pass them on the side that takes the wind from their sales. Taking the sails down is trying to put in positive things or things that would help make everyone OK, and at the same time get through difficult times and survive the storm or difficult period.

It's like a self-fulfilling prophesy, the more we get caught up into destructive systems, the more the destructive systems win. The most productive situation requires a courageous, thinking, creative, confident person.

One might ask, what happens if a bully picks on you? Either leave or if really confronted, use the basic principles to obtain every means to negotiate a positive outcome for all. Of course, this takes us right to the issue of maturity. To be mature is to embrace five different concepts: being kind, caring, understanding, firm and able to "deal with." A mature person isn't just about age; it is being able to fully develop these five different characteristics.

- Kind - Being kind-hearted

- Care - Being a caring person (e.g., I care about what is going on, I care about working toward the best outcome possible)

- Understand - understanding is I'm willing to comprehend as best as I can

- Firm – I will hold strongly to the beliefs that I have

- "Deal With" – I am willing to deal with those things and other new ideas that help us negotiate with each other.

Let's look at one of the basic five concepts we've talked about where new information provides opportunity for renegotiation. Care is a good one. To Care – there is a gender factor here. The best way to explain it is when a child decides to get a

Chapter 15

---

motorcycle the father says "Yes" even though he knows the child could sustain a broken arm or a severe injury. The mother goes into a deep nurture and may say to the father "You handle it." Because the mother is an intuitive and nurturing person she sees the child splattered all over the highway. So there is a difference based on gender regarding caring. Caring is rather complex, it is not just I care; there are various other factors that go into it. "I care to work with you and I care that we work this out together."

CHAPTER 16

Concentrate on the Positive

In looking only at what is destructive or what we might call negative or evil, is the self-fulfilling prophecy. Let me give an example, if you are in a cow pasture there is a high likelihood that there is manure. Now you just noticed that you stepped in it. There are some alternative ways to handle this. You can be upset that you stepped in the cow manure, and so you step in it more and keep stepping in it. Another approach is though you notice it, you walk right through it but it stays on your shoes; thus you just end up spreading the manure wherever you go. The other option is of course to go, clean it off, and go on. But, there is a fourth step, and that is turning a negative into something positive. For example, putting the cow manure into a manure spreader as fertilizer for some plants is turning what can be negative into something good.

Chapter 16

So you've got to know what you are doing but you can turn negative things into positive things. Again, you are not standing and stomping in it, or carrying it around with you, instead you are doing something about it. If all that you are focusing on is what's negative, then you stay tangled in its effect.

I use the illustration of what I call "a jeep in the desert." You're driving, it's a beautiful day, you are having a wonderful time, can go anywhere you want to go, and you just feel free. Then you see a speck in the distance and as you go along you see that it is a pile of rocks. You can look at it and say "I'm not going to hit it; I'm not going to hit it." Next thing you know the pile of rocks is right in front of you. So what happens is we think I'm not going to get involved, I'm not going to get involved. Therefore we are only focusing one the one thing that is not working. The best thing to do is stop the jeep, identify and acknowledge they are rocks, knowing that if you continue in that direction you could crash into them. So you look at the horizon and see a little bit of green. Head for the green, go down the deep slope and up the sand dune and start down, and there is another pile of rocks. Knowing that rocks are in the area, you can continue to focus on the oasis and find a way around the rocks and continue to work toward the best outcome. That means; define what would be in the best interest.

In summary, one of the ways to avoid staying caught up in what's negative is to look at what could be put in its place and then you present that as a positive solution. If people focus on what is negative they inadvertently create more negative. It takes courage to present and to focus on other things because often you can be accused of knowing it all or you are accused that you always want it your way. You can use the approach asking the other person to give you some ideas of how it would work for all of us – for you and me, and I will be glad to consider it and that you are willing to look at any new knowledge. If there is no new knowledge, it would be in the best interest for all of us to consider available options. Acknowledge what is not working, and be thinking about what does work and work toward them. Ultimately you get past the rocks.

By the way, the word "accept" is a strange word because it tends to mean, "I'm supposed to find a way to like it." Just accept it – and many times, it is "just accept the fact you lost your job, just accept the fact that your spouse left you, you

Chapter 16

need to find a way to accept it to be able to forget it and go on with your life. Implying "accept" means "having to like" is a mistake. The word "acknowledge" is a word that really sets the stage for us to be able to go on. I know the place with the rocks, I acknowledge the rocks, the loss, the grief, and identify it for what it is... and then I look at those things I can do to deal with it. I can now go on toward continuing the goal of adding on to life and preserving life in a positive way.

In this complex society, it is no longer a situation of being weak when one searches all of the resources possible for resolving any given problem. It is important to remember that it takes a complex answer to resolve any complex problem in a complex society. As a matter of fact, it is actually a source of personal strength when an individual is willing to pursue all possible resources in order to strive for human happiness and potential, not only for themselves, but also for others around them and in society in general.

CHAPTER 17

What to Do Now!

It is important that we change the elements of physical survival, which we are taught from the academic classroom, to these new concepts. If we do, we would have a renewed social system that is no longer structured on punishment. Instead, we would be looking toward knowing, being, becoming and discovering what is new. We would be thinking, willing to add on, efficient, effective and responsible.

HISTORICAL	NOW!
Only socially assigned authorities are "right"	All authorities can be considered
Personal creativity is inhibited	Individual and group creativity is encouraged
Learning and obeying the rules without questioning is essential	Self-thinking is developed
	Internalization is promoted
Externalization is essential (Do what you are told to do)	Pro-action is encouraged
Reaction is learned Dependency is necessary until "right" behavior is achieved	Inter-dependency is an outcome; therefore, maturity is more readily achieved

Chapter 17

Margaret Meade talks about "now is the future." This means that what we operate as now predicts the next now. What we do now fits in our complex society in that now I can be a responsible person and that whatever is done predicts the best possible outcome now. It includes the best efficiency and effectiveness in working toward the ability to respond.

This helps increase batting averages, encourages knowing everything we can know to learn and to grow, adds-on, and then finally, includes the last statement of:

"The more I know, the more I find out there is more to know"
– how exciting life can be!"

APPENDIX A

LISTENING

"I know that you believe you understand what you think I said, but I am not sure you realize that what you heard is not what I meant!"

Just Listen!

"It's simple, when I ask you to listen to me and you
start giving advice, you have not done
what I asked.

When I ask you to listen to me and you begin to tell
me why I shouldn't feel that way, you are
trampling on my feelings.

When I ask you to listen to me and you feel you
have to do something to solve my problem,
you have failed me, strange as that may seem.

Appendix A

Listen!

All I ask is that you listen, not talk or
do – just listen, hear me.
Advice is cheap – 50 cents will get you
both Dear Abby and Billy Graham in the same
newspaper. I can do for myself; I'm not
helpless, maybe discouraged and faltering,
but not helpless.

When you do something for me that I can
and need to do for myself, you contribute
to my fear and weakness.

But, when you acknowledge as a simple
fact that I do feel what I feel, no matter
how irrational, then I can quit trying
to convince you and can get about the
business of understanding what is behind
this irrational feeling. And when that's
clear, the answers are obvious and
I don't need advice.

Irrational feelings make sense when
we understand what's behind them.

So, please just listen and just hear me.
And, if you want to talk,
wait a minute for your turn;
and then *I'll listen to you!"*

To listen and to help someone hear himself or herself is a learning experience for all participants. Understanding emerges and the outcome is not pre-perceived. The goal is to change the "listen *to tell*" ear to a "listen to *listen and understand*" ear.

A 10 Minute Exercise

- Pick a topic starting with:
    - "I remember when ..."
    - "When I was a kid ..."
    - "I've always liked to ..."
    - "Fun times I had were ..."

- Using strict timing, each person spends five minutes to say what they would like to say or how they feel about the topic.

- Flip a coin to see who goes first.

- No one is to reflect or comment on the other person's responses.

- If the person talking doesn't talk five minutes, only change speakers after their five minutes' time is up.

Appendix A

- The listener observes the speaker's non-verbal messages as well as verbal.

- The listener never speaks and will not respond to what is said, but is responsible for concentrating on what the other person says and his non-verbal behavior.

- The listener concentrates on content, body language, and feelings that are communicated. Try not to make any approval or disapproval responses non-verbally.

- The object is to listen with your mind and feeling sensors.

- Since each person is free of reacting or giving feedback when listening, no one needs to be thinking of what might be said back and can concentrate on what is being communicated.

After this experience the topic is not to be discussed. Both are to move to another activity, individually or together.

The goal is to own one's own feelings and what has been shared. The speaker experiences

Listening

what it is like to be truly heard. The listener experiences the tools required to stop and listen to another's conversation without consciously or subconsciously thinking about what to say or how to respond.

After practicing this exercise a few times the listener will start becoming a better listener and will experience a new alertness to the speaker and what is being communicated. Have fun with this. This is an exercise for growth and learning. Enjoy each other's conversations and then go out into the world and see if you see changes in other's responses as you listen to them!

Advanced Reflective Listening

This is the "in-depth communication system" used after the 10 Minute Exercise becomes comfortable. One person speaks, while the other person acts as a mirror or reflector, giving the speaker the opportunity to clarify and rephrase until a clear understanding is achieved. The main purpose of this exercise is to continue learning how to listen as well as to experience the basic notion of owning one's own feelings. Insight, using the following perception clarification tools, provides for a better understanding and better action.

Appendix A

General Guidelines:

- To begin, pick a subject. Then *stick to the subject*. For the purpose of this exercise, pick a subject that is of interest to both parties. Each party will play the listener and then will switch and play the speaker.

- <u>Do not interject one's own judgment, comments, or ideas if you are the listener</u>. Only reflect, echo or mirror words, ideas or feelings you sense or hear from the speaker.

- Think in a positive and constructive manner. Remind yourself that the objective is to work toward agreement, to consider one's own feelings as well as the other's, and that it is important to complete the exercise – mentally, emotionally, and physically. Stand strong, be united, defend each other and enjoy this new learning and growing experience.

- If, during this exercise your feelings start running too high use the STOP TOOL *(below)*.

▶ As the listener, ask for clarification to understand feelings or unclear words that result from the following:
- One's own thoughts or feelings.
- The other person's word usage or non-verbal innuendos.
- The other person's feelings that are detected.
- One's own or the other person's actions.

▶ As the listener use statements such as:
- "Help me understand."
- "What I hear you saying is ..."
- "You seem to be saying ..."
- "I sense that you are feeling ..."
- "I'm not sure, maybe it's me, but I am feeling ... (uncomfortable, hurt, concerned, etc.)"

▶ Refrain from statements such as:
- "That's wrong."
- "You're wrong."
- "You shouldn't."
- "I know how you feel ... "
- "You don't mean that."
- "I know you ..."
- "If ... then..."

Appendix A

- ▶ Change speakers by one of the following two ways:
    - The listener saying, "I am beginning to feel uneasy (confused, uncertain, upset, etc.) and I'm not sure exactly why. Would you help me understand this?" (In other words, "Please change places with me.")
    - The speaker saying, "I'm still not sure I've been understood," or "Yes, give me some feedback," or "I feel you understood me well, let's change and I'll reflect."

If understanding is indicated by both parties via feedback, then negotiation can take place on the basis of the following concept: "In light of new and present knowledge, I am willing to stay with past decisions or to state new positions." *Or*, if negotiation is not possible at this time, stop the session. Stay positive that the creative growth that is being experienced will eventually produce resolutions.

It takes time to learn how to listen and reflect. Once each person has enough insight, resolutions can be reached. In the meantime, one can always decide not to decide.

Listening

> ## STOP TOOL
>
> *The person that is feeling too much is happening says, "STOP" or "Time Out." This means, "I care about us enough to not want hurt to occur." The person saying stop gets coffee, takes a break, or does something positive about the situation. Both participate and change the subject, situation, location (for example, go for a walk, etc.).*
>
> *Note: Each must agree to a new time and place in which the subject will again be discussed.*

This "in-depth communication system" takes into account the concept that change is constant. In light of new knowledge I act while continuing acting on "in light of present knowledge."
Each time one experiences new knowledge or understanding, it creates a new situation. In this new system new decisions can be made so that no one has to "lose face." In addition to the fact that change is okay, it is also okay to make a mistake!

To be wrong is to be "less than" a person (or a less than perfect person). Our current goal is to be perfect and make 100%. To correct one's self while continuing to gain new knowledge and insight provides the ability to redirect and

Appendix A

determine what is right for the situation. The alternative is to revert to the old punishment model. We must think of our mistakes as actions that can be corrected without punishment. This new thinking signals that things are not working but that through the help of self, others, books, etc., one can gain new insight to correct the situation. Sometimes the mistake itself gives us insight as to what further actions are best.

Remember, mistakes are okay. Just act – or sometimes choose not to act – until you are ready or until all of the facts are in to the degree that action can start in a more confident manner. You see, perception is usually the problem; therefore no one is to blame. The goal is to know. Guilt causes us to be stuck.

Each day begin to use the following words less and less:		
Don't	Ought to	You better
Wrong	Right to	A direct "You ...!"
Should	Have to	Always
Shouldn't	Must	Never

APPENDIX B

CHANGING IRRATIONAL "SELF-DOWNING" TALK TO RATIONAL "SELF-APPROVAL" TALK

Event: An event occurs, such as meeting with someone or having a disagreement with someone, or an accident, etc.

Results of Event: After the event there can be a reaction, response or consequence which creates negative feelings. Examples include anxious feelings due to the person we met who didn't speak to us or put us down, or bad feelings due to a disagreement or an argument. The situation may result in angry or hurt feelings toward the person or situation, or in the case of an accident – not only are you upset, but also your car is ruined.

Self-Downing Talk: This tends to be what we say to ourselves when a negative experience occurs

Appendix B

that we feel we did not resolve, or handle well. The desire to be perfect, to be 100%, to be right in order to be a worthwhile person seems to take over, or the desire to be "more" perfect by admitting how wrong we were.

For example:

- "It's terrible that I am anxious or can't understand or didn't respond correctly."

- "It's awful that things didn't work out the way they should have."

- "Anyone who was worth anything wouldn't have these feelings or would have handled the situation better."

- "I feel awful."

- "If I were really capable I'd have not gotten into this fix."

- "It's awful."

- "It's terrible."

- "I'm awful"

- "I have a headache."

- "Why don't others understand and help or leave me alone?"

- "I must not be worth it."

Changing Irrational "Self-Downing" Talk to Rational "Self-Approval" Talk

- "I'm worthless."
- "It's always my fault that things don't work out."
- "Why can't I prevent these unpleasant things from happening?"
- "I must really be inadequate."
- "I'm not much of a person after all."
- "My stomach hurts."
- "I feel sick."
- "I'm depressed."
- "Nobody cares."
- "I don't care."
- "Why even try?"
- "Life isn't worth it."
- "Why must I suffer so?"

Self-Approval Talk: To keep from irrational self-downing talk, Albert Ellis, author of A New Guide to Rational Living, suggests saying the following. Repeat these three statements until they become automatic to you.

1. "I don't like it!"

2. "I don't have to like it!"

3. "I'll do what's in my power to change it. If it is out of my power, and change isn't happening at this time ... it can be tough ... but ... I'm still a worthwhile person!"

There is a popular opinion that says we should like bad things since those things, if overcome, help build character ... or we learn that if it is hard it must be worth it, no pain no gain. This is a fallacy. You do not have to like the bad event; it is how you choose to respond to the event that will build character and self-esteem.

Just being a person causes one to be worthwhile. We grow; we make mistakes and continue to grow when we recognize that we are worthwhile. Remember, a mistake is simply a misdirected action, not knowing what else to do at the time. One is not bad or "less than" to make a mistake.

Get back on Target and Begin to Problem Solve: The following steps are suggested to help you move toward a positive response that also results in self-approval and awareness.

Changing Irrational "Self-Downing" Talk to Rational "Self-Approval" Talk

1. Ask the question: "What is so terrible or awful?"
2. Respond to: "It is just awful that _____ _____, or _____, or _____ _____, etc.
3. There may be more than one response. Write each response down.
4. Select one of the above topics and use it to practice creative decision-making.

Creative Decision Making: Each of the above topics can be used in sequence as you so choose. It is generally best to select the topic with the least emotional impact and progress on to a topic that is more difficult.

1. Place the topic you have selected at the top left hand corner of a piece of paper. Make two columns on your page next to the topic. At the top of the first column put – Brainstorming Action Alternatives. At the top of the second column put – Brainstorming Possible Consequences. Now go through and list all of the possible actions that you can think of under the Alternatives column. These need not be actions that are absolutely possible. They may be positive or negative. When listing possible actions,

Appendix B

---

assume that all of the resources are or will be available. This process is what frees one from a former mind set. It is often hard to break a mind set, or a way that we have been doing something in the past. This is generally what causes us to continue in a vicious circle and come up with very few ideas for action. The suggestion given here is for the purpose of breaking that mind set and considering the possibility of other kinds of possible action(s).

2. When you have completed the Alternatives action column, go to the next column. Start again at the top of the page. After each action, list the possible consequences for each action under the Possible Consequences heading. It is probably best if you leave space between the actions that you have listed so that you will have room to write quite a few consequences for each action. After each action has a possible consequence(s) listed, you will be able to take the last step.

3. Place a piece of paper over the possible actions, showing only the column of consequences. Number the consequences

in highest priority. For example, the consequence you like the most, number that one and on down. Then on another piece of paper, see if you can combine 1, 2, 3 or 4 consequences. Once you have determined the consequences you may prefer a combination of consequences. Take your sheet of paper away from the possible courses of action and follow those actions related to the desired consequences as best as possible in the most desirable sequence. It may be that you move on in a systematic way as you feel comfortable with an action, or as you feel you can handle an action at the present time. Secondly, reality kinds of things will now enter the picture; for example, if costs are involved, is it possible to handle that with your present financial situation? Or, if it is an action that you'd prefer taking after other actions, begin with one in which you can answer the following questions:

- Out of fairness to myself ...
- In light of present knowledge ...
- Owning my own feelings ...
- Am I am working toward agreement or cooperation?
- Have I used all resources, including myself?

Appendix B

Summary: When an individual meets a particular situation and uses *self-downing* talk, which moves one into a state of depression, *self-approval* talk can be selected with the statement "I will do what is in my power to change things." Through the creative decision making process one can find that there are many actions to take. With this in mind, a person can be self-directed and can take action. This emphasizes that one is a unique person. The person also finds many other resources available if willing to search out such things in the forms of books, other people, libraries, or professionals. It also enhances positive self-concept.

In this complex society, it is no longer a situation of being weak when one searches all of the resources possible for resolving any given problem. It is important to remember that it takes a complex answer to resolve any in-depth complex problem in a complex society. As a matter of fact, it is actually a source of personal strength when people are willing to pursue all possible resources in order to strive for human happiness, not only for themselves, but also for others around them and in society in general.

APPENDIX C

RULES, ROLES & BOUNDARIES

R is for the Right way to play
U is for the Ugly remarks we must not say
L is for the Limits we'll set and try to obey
E is for the Equal time we'll give day to day
S is for the Sharing in each and every way

R is not for Ruling the other
O is not for Obstructing the other
L is not for Lording over the other
E is not for Evading the other
S is not for Shaming the other

B will be for Belts we won't hit below
O will be for important issues we'll Outline
U will be for trying to Understanding each other
N will be for Not being Narrow minded
D will be for Danger zones we'll avoid
A will be for sensitive Areas to remember
R will be for Remembering each other's wants
I will be for Imaginary lines we'll draw
E will be for Emphasizing what we need
S will be for Space we'll give each other

APPENDIX D

SCRIPTURE REFERENCES

Scriptures for reflection, meditation and encouragement *(taken from the New American Standard Bible)*:

- Psalms 133:1
- Proverbs 1:5
- Proverbs 14:15
- Proverbs 14:29
- Proverbs 15:1,2
- Proverbs 22:6
- Mark 12:31
- John 3:16
- I Corinthians 13
- Ephesians 4:32
- Philippians 4:8
- Colossians 3:8-10
- Colossians 3:21
- Colossians 4:6
- James 1:5
- James 1:19

APPENDIX E

ABOUT THE AUTHOR

George Franklin Rosselot

OVERVIEW

Professional Work Experience:

Founder, Owner and Executive Director of Eastwood Clinic, Inc., Tallahassee, Florida, with a full-time private practice as a Marriage and Family Therapist from 1973-2004. Director and Associate Professor at Florida A&M University and Director of Upward Bound, which targeted high-risk and high potential students who were underachievers from 1969-1974. Experience includes over 50 years of working in the areas of private practice, guidance counseling, education, social services, youth programs and ministry. In addition, Mr. Rosselot produced and hosted television programs in Tallahassee and Cleveland that dealt with social problems confronting adolescents and young adults.

Appendix E

Education:

M.S. Education, University of Akron; Post-Graduate work at Kent State University; B.S. Education, Indianapolis University; Doctoral course work and residency requirements fulfilled in Adult Education and Marriage and Family Therapy, Florida State University. Pastoral Theology course work at United Theological Seminary.

Clinical Experience:

Individual, Marriage and Family, Adolescent Psychotherapy, Divorce and Mediation Therapy, Rehabilitation and Career Counseling, Youth Ministry and Theological Counseling, Educational Television Production, Educational Consulting.

Professional Affiliations:

American Association of Marriage and Family Therapy, Past President of Florida Association of Marriage and Family Therapy, American Counseling Association, Florida Mental Health Counseling Association, American Association of Sex Educators, Counselors, and Therapists.

Licenses Held:

Licensed Marriage and Family Therapist, State of Florida: MT 0000001; Licensed School Psychologist, State of Florida: SS 0000049; Licensed Mental Health Counselor, State of Florida: MH 0000202.

Areas of Special Interest:

Marriage and Family Therapy, Adolescent and Young Adult Therapy, Gender Identity Issues; Human Sexuality and Education Counseling, Women's Traumas, Career and Psycho-Educational Consulting, Divorce Adjustment, Parent Education, Grief Therapy, Consulting in Organizational Systems, Spiritual Life Development.

Personal Background:

George Rosselot was born in Kokomo, Indiana in 1931. He was reared in Sierra Leone, West Africa. His parents were missionaries in West Africa until 1939 when the family returned to the State of Indiana. Mr. Rosselot has maintained personal relationships to this day with African leaders and friends. In addition to his illustrious career, he also pioneered in over 15 extensive Youth Educational Study Trips which spanned a period of nine years. The experience included extensive travel throughout the United States. This program included

Appendix E

---

working with a diverse group of individuals and ethnic organizations as well as various religious groups and cultures.

Current Information:

Mr. Rosselot is currently semi-retired and living with his wife of 54 years, Shirley M. Rosselot. They reside in Tallahassee, Florida and have four children, three grandchildren, and three great-grand children. In his own words he has not retired, rather, he has "re-wired" and is now engaged in writing and publishing several books that have been in development over the past 30 years from concepts developed through his clinical therapy and professional practice.

About the Author

LEGISLATIVE INVOLVEMENT

George Rosselot began working with licensure for Marriage and Family Therapists in 1974 as Legislative Chair for the Florida Association for Marriage and Family Therapy (FAMFT) and Florida Mental Health Counselors. He played a primary role in drafting the first law (1983) and revised the law effective in 1988. He was President of FAMFT, served on the American Association for Marriage and Family Therapy Committee (AAMFT) for Legislative Grants, and was honored as a Fellow by AAMFT for his legislative accomplishments establishing Marriage and Family Therapy as a profession by State Law. He received recognition for outstanding leadership at the AAMFT National Convention in 1986, was issued the first Marriage and Family Therapy license by the Florida Department of Professional Regulation (DPR) honoring his accomplishments with regard to the first licensing of Marriage and Family Therapists in the State, served as consultant to DPR for rule making and examination development for Florida Marriage and Family Therapists, and was elected Chair of Division II Presidents Council. He has been called on as a consultant by AAMFT administrators and various division leaders.

Appendix E

In 1973, he founded a private interdisciplinary group practice in Tallahassee, Florida. As a clinician in full time private practice, he has dealt with the complex issues where law, regulation, and intraprofessional systems mesh at a grass roots level. He was one of the pioneers to activate and design a Coalition of Interdisciplinary Professionals within the State of Florida. He has extensive understanding and experience in the political arena involving legislative and intraprofessional issues.

In 1992 he was a key leader encouraging lawmakers to place Marriage and Family Therapists, Clinical Social Workers and Mental Health Counselors in the Judicial Evidence Code defining each as a Psychotherapist with confidentiality as stated in the State Evidence Code. He also assisted with the professional law change providing that 490 and 491 Chapters be a "Practice Act" defining each profession therein, thus increasing the Florida Standards of Psychologists, School Psychologists, Clinical Social Workers, Marriage and Family Therapists, and Mental Health Counselors who formerly held only title protection.

Mr. Rosselot holds firm to his primary philosophy that the "Best Interest of the Public" must always be first and foremost regarding professionalism, services provided, ethics, and especially law and regulatory rules.

www.ingramcontent.com/pod-product-compliance
Lightning Source LLC
Chambersburg PA
CBHW031249290426
44109CB00012B/505